Henry L. Dempsey
Albany Feb 26th 1866

1865.
STATE OF NEW YORK.

PRESENTATION OF FLAGS

OF

NEW YORK VOLUNTEER REGIMENTS

AND OTHER ORGANIZATIONS, TO

HIS EXCELLENCY, GOVERNOR FENTON,

IN ACCORDANCE WITH A RESOLUTION OF THE LEGISLATURE,

JULY 4, 1865.

PUBLISHED UNDER DIRECTION OF THE
CHIEF OF BUREAU OF MILITARY RECORD.

THIS WORK IS DEDICATED

TO THE

𝔙olunteer 𝔗roops from the 𝔖tate of 𝔑ew 𝔜ork,

IN

TESTIMONY OF THEIR DEVOTION

TO

OUR COMMON COUNTRY.

HIS EXCELLENCY,

REUBEN E. FENTON,

GOVERNOR,

COMMANDER-IN-CHIEF OF THE STATE OF NEW YORK.

PRIVATE SECRETARY,
GEORGE S. HASTINGS.

HIS HONOR,

THOMAS G. ALVORD,

LIEUT.-GOVERNOR.

STAFF:

ADJUTANT-GENERAL,
BRIGADIER-GEN. WILLIAM IRVINE.

INSPECTOR-GENERAL,
BRIGADIER-GEN. GEORGE S. BATCHELLER.

ENGINEER-IN-CHIEF,
BRIGADIER-GEN. JAMES B. SWAIN.

JUDGE-ADVOCATE-GENERAL,
BRIGADIER-GEN. ALEXANDER W. HARVEY.

COMMISSARY-GENERAL OF ORDNANCE,
BRIGADIER-GEN. FRANK CHAMBERLAIN.

SURGEON-GENERAL,
BRIGADIER-GEN. JAMES L. POMFRET.

QUARTERMASTER-GENERAL,
BRIGADIER-GEN. EDWIN A. MERRITT.

PAYMASTER-GENERAL,
BRIGADIER-GEN. SELDEN E. MARVIN.

AID-DE-CAMPS,
COLONEL   MICHAEL J. FARRELL.
COLONEL   DELAVAN G. MORGAN.

MILITARY SECRETARY,
COLONEL   JOHN MANLEY.

CHIEF OF BUREAU OF MILITARY RECORD,
COLONEL   LOCKWOOD L. DOTY.

INTRODUCTORY.

THE Bureau of Military Record was established by an order of Governor MORGAN, in December, 1862. At the following session the measure received the sanction of the Legislature, and has since been continued by the authority of that body.

The objects of the Bureau are to collect and preserve the records of the war, and, especially, 1. The biographies of officers and men engaged in the service from this State. 2. Detailed accounts of the organization and services of Regiments and other organizations, including the history and the preservation of their flags. 3. The action of Towns, Cities and Counties in raising volunteers and in contributing to the aid of Sanitary and other commissions, and to the support of families of soldiers. 4. The collection of printed documents and papers, sermons, pamphlets, &c., as well as the various matters connected with the war that would otherwise be without an official repository.

In the prosecution of these objects the Bureau has met with no little success. A large majority of the Regiments that have been raised in the State, are already represented by one or more of their flags—no less than five hundred having been placed in its custody; biographies of many officers and men have been received, and a thorough canvass of the State is now being made for the collection of statistical and other information.

The Legislature of 1865, extended the duties of the Bureau to the collection and preservation of "a record of the part taken by seamen from this State, in the naval service, since the beginning of the war," and also to the procuring of "a detailed account of the treatment of Union soldiers from this State, in rebel prisons, and a record of the deaths in said prisons, and other pertinent facts connected with such imprisonment." These additional divisions have been organized and are now prosecuting the work assigned to them.

In connection with the Bureau a museum of articles of military interest has been established, which seeks additions from all sources.

The rapidly increasing materials deposited in the Bureau, and their historic value, were considered by the Legislature at its last session, and an act was passed "to provide a suitable repository for the records of the war, and for other purposes." The Commissioners named in this act, viz.: The GOVERNOR, the LIEUTENANT-GOVERNOR, the CHANCELLOR OF THE UNIVERSITY, JOHN A. KING, HAMILTON FISH, EDWIN D. MORGAN, JOHN A. DIX, IRA HARRIS, PRESTON KING, HORATIO SEYMOUR, DANIEL S. DICKINSON, ENOS T. THROOP, MYRON H. CLARK, WASHINGTON HUNT, MILLARD FILLMORE, and the CHIEF OF THE BUREAU, have already taken measures which, it is confidently believed, will result in the erection of a fire-proof edifice to be called THE HALL OF MILITARY RECORD.

The active co-operation of officers and soldiers who have been or may now be in the service is solicited in increasing the collections already begun, to the end that every officer and soldier may have here an appropriate record; that every flag that has represented the State in the field may be returned and preserved; that every Regiment may have a history of its services, and every town and city a memorial of its efforts to uphold the arms of the government in preserving the unity of the nation and the principles which animated its founders.

Suitable blanks for any of these purposes may be obtained by addressing the Chief of the Bureau.

All communications or donations should be addressed to

LOCKWOOD L. DOTY,
Chief of Bureau of Military Record,
Albany, N. Y.

PROCEEDINGS OF THE LEGISLATURE.

STATE OF NEW YORK,
IN ASSEMBLY, ALBANY, *April* 28, 1865.

On motion of Mr. J. L. PARKER,

Resolved (if the Senate concur), That the Flags of New York Volunteer Regiments deposited in the Bureau of Military Statistics, be publicly presented on the Fourth of July next, and that His Excellency, the Governor, be and he hereby is requested to receive them on behalf of the State at that time.

Resolved, That the Chief of the said Bureau be directed and he hereby is directed, to prepare a brief history of such Flags, to be used on that occasion, and that he also prepare an account of the proceedings on that occasion, including the brief histories, and that 1,500 copies thereof, in pamphlet form, be printed, 1,000 for the Legislature and 500 for the Chief of Bureau.

By order of the Assembly.

J. B. CUSHMAN, *Clerk.*

IN SENATE, *April* 28, 1865.

The foregoing resolution was duly passed.

By order,

JAS. TERWILLIGER, *Clerk.*

CORRESPONDENCE.

In reply to invitations, letters were received from Lieut.-Gen. WINFIELD SCOTT, Maj.-Gens. JOHN E. WOOL, JOHN A. DIX, JOSEPH HOOKER, H. W. SLOCUM, JNO. S. RAWLINS, and H. E. DAVIES, JR., and Col. JOHN T. SPRAGUE, of the army, and from Vice-Admiral D. G. FARRAGUT of the navy. Invitations were also replied to by Judges of the Court of Appeals, Officers of the State, Members of the Legislature, and others.

LETTER FROM LIEUT.-GENERAL WINFIELD SCOTT.

WEST POINT, N. Y., *June 30, 1865.*
To His Excellency, R. E. FENTON,
Governor of New York:

Dear Sir—I am sensibly affected by your kind and flattering invitation to be present, at Albany, on the approaching National Anniversary, to witness the consecration to fame of the New York flags, which her noble volunteers bore in triumph in concert with the troops of other conservative States, over so many bloody fields up to the full restoration of our glorious Union. Please accept my apology for declining the honor tendered me, for, though slowly improving in health, I am still wanting in the strength to bear much fatigue of body or excitement of mind.

With high respect,
I have the honor to be
Your Excellency's ob't servant,
WINFIELD SCOTT.

LETTER FROM VICE-ADMIRAL D. G. FARRAGUT.

BROOKLYN NAVY YARD, *June* 29, 1865.

To L. L. DOTY, *Chief of Bureau:*

Owing to the uncertainty of my movements, your kind invitation to be present at the return of the regimental flags to the public authorities of the State, only reached me yesterday, and found me already engaged by the Mayor of Boston, to be present at the 4th July celebration there. Will you therefore accept this excuse for my not being at Albany on so interesting an occasion, and will you please express my thanks to His Excellency, Gov. FENTON, and to the Legislature for the honor they have bestowed upon me by the invitation?

Very respectfully,
Your obedient servant,
D. G. FARRAGUT,
Vice-Admiral.

PRESENTATION CEREMONIES.

The ceremony of presenting the Flags to His Excellency, the Governor, was conducted in connection with the public celebration of the Anniversary of American Independence by the Young Men's Association of Albany, in a spacious building erected for that purpose on Washington Parade Ground. The stage was occupied by Governor FENTON and Staff, and Members of the Legislature, and by the following, among other invited guests, viz.:

>Lieut.-General U. S. GRANT and Staff,
>Major-General JOHN E. WOOL,
>Major-General LEWIS WALLACE,
>Major-General JUDSON KILPATRICK,
>Major-General JOHN A. SCHOFIELD,
>Major-General DANIEL BUTTERFIELD,
>Major-General DANIEL E. SICKLES,
>Major-General JOHN J. PECK,
>Major-General JAMES B. RICKETTS,
>Major-General JAMES C. ROGERS,
>Major-General —— COGSWELL,
>Major-General JOHN TAYLER COOPER,
>Brig.-General JOHN C. ROBINSON,
>Brig.-General PATRICK H. JONES,

  Brig.-General IRA SPAULDING,
  Brig.-General SAMUEL H. ROBERTS,
  Brig.-General AUGUSTUS V. KAUTZ,
  Brig.-General THOMAS C. DEVIN,
  Brig.-General JOHN T. SPRAGUE,
  Judge   HENRY E. DAVIES,
  Judge   PLATT POTTER,
  Judge   WILLIAM W. CAMPBELL.

The exercises were opened with prayer by Rev. J. LIVINGSTON REESE.

After music, General J. MEREDITH READ, Jr., read the Declaration of Independence.

Major-General DANIEL BUTTERFIELD then delivered the Presentation Address, which was responded to by His Excellency Governor FENTON.

The Flags were then presented, with brief histories.

Rev. E. H. CHAPIN, D. D., followed with the Oration.

Major-General DANIEL E. SICKLES, in response to calls, delivered a few remarks.

The exercises were closed by Benediction pronounced by Rev. Mr. BRIDGMAN.

The addresses, &c., are given in their order.

PRAYER,

BY REV. J. LIVINGSTON REESE.

ALMIGHTY GOD, our Heavenly Father, who art a most strong tower to those who put their trust in Thee, to whom all things in heaven, in earth and under the earth do bow and obey, we yield Thee most hearty praise and thanksgiving for Thy great and undeserved goodness to the people of this land. We have heard with our ears and our fathers have declared unto us the noble works Thou didst in their days, and in the old time before them. We praise Thee for these memories of the past, for the good examples of Thy servants by whose faith and patriotism our national union was established, under which this people, by Thy providence, have been so signally prospered and blessed. And now, O Sovereign Lord, on this day especially, when Thou didst put it into the hearts of our fathers to establish this nation as a free and independent people, we would bless and magnify Thy glorious name that Thou hast in our own time stretched forth Thy hand and been our Saviour and mighty deliverer. We acknowledge that it was Thy arm that brought salvation, and Thy strength that gave deliverance. Give, O Lord, we beseech Thee, to all such as are intrusted with the government and defense of this nation, Thy most gracious support and guidance. Make Thy word to be their light and Thine arm their strength. O God, Holy Ghost, sanctifier of the faithful, visit them, we pray Thee, and this whole nation with Thy love and favor; enlighten their minds more and more with the light of the everlasting Gospel; graft in their hearts a love of the truth; increase in them true religion; nourish them with all goodness and of Thy great mercy keep them in the same, O blessed Spirit, whom with the Father and the Son together we worship and glorify as one God. World without end. Amen.

PRESENTATION ADDRESS,

BY MAJ.-GENERAL DANIEL BUTTERFIELD, U. S. A.

Your Excellency, Senators, Members of Assembly and Citizens: I am requested to present you these flags in behalf of your soldiers, who have borne them with courage and honor in the changing fortunes of battle. Many of these regiments are not represented here save by these and the joy that fills our hearts at the success of our arms, for of that success they are part.

Their heroic deeds would fill volumes. Time will not permit that I should recount them here. The brave hearts that yielded life whilst bearing these banners in defense of liberty; the majesty of the law; the safety, honor and welfare of country, are buried on every field of our recent conflict. From the Susquehanna to the Potomac, from the Potomac to the James, from the James to the Roanoke, from the Shenandoah to the Cumberland, from the Cumberland to the Tennessee; through the Mississippi Valley, east and west, to the Alabama and Rio Grande, from the Tennessee to the Chattahoochie, from the Chattahoochie to the Savannah, and from the Savannah back to the Roanoke—the mighty rivers that flow to the Gulf and Atlantic—have been crimsoned with patriot blood. The plains, the valleys and the mountain sides hold the honored dead who fought our battles. Their names and fame are recorded for all time in the archives of your government; their memories are enshrined in the hearts of a grateful people.

These standards are returned, battle-scarred, hallowed by the blood of your patriot sons — a precious treasure, a priceless legacy, for they shall tell your children's children of manhood and patriotism rising in their might to sustain the right. These are glorious insignia of the highest devotion and sacrifice of man for man, of man for country. I need not ask you to cherish them proudly. I may ask you, since by the aid of Almighty God, the valor of our arms has achieved such signal success, that you cherish them without revenge, cherish them only as proud mementoes of the triumph of right.

The war is at an end. That brave and noble chieftain who led our armies to victory in the field, prescribed the terms by which the conquered foe might rest. Vested with full power, where war by force of arms had superseded civil law, your chosen general told the fallen enemy: "Lay down your arms, obey the law, and war shall end — you are unmolested during good behavior." Do you ask vengeance? The brave are ever generous. Vengeance for the best blood of our youth spilled beneath the folds of these historic banners! Then bid the disarmed foe to live amid the scenes of desolation and woe wrought by his treason — to live with the horrible recollection of thousands of brave, loyal men brought to nakedness, hunger, famine, idiocy and death by their cruel imprisonment. Thus to live only to pray for death's relief from such a life.

The names of those traitors, who, children of our common country — educated, trained and nurtured by it — honored with its sword, bound to it by manhood's oath — the names of these shall go down forever in your history, companions in infamy with BENEDICT ARNOLD'S. They are punished. Let them go. *Rather than the implied faith and honor of the nation should be broken, better all should escape.*

The offended majesty of the civil law may deal justly with those traitors, who, honored with place and power at the hands of an innocent, confiding people, used these gifts for years to plant the germ of treason, in the vain attempt to overthrow this government, that slavery, despotism and sin might thrive upon its ruin. Saddened hearts and lonely hearth-stones in our land, mourning our martyred chief and fallen heroes, victims alike of such treason, ask rather in sorrow than in anger, that these should meet with justice, a warning to those who would hereafter force civilized government from the hands of a free people, to rest upon bayonets, "bed rock" of that civilization where men are no longer free.

All wars are waged for principle or interest. Adhering to the principles in defense of which we have drawn the sword, let us turn to reconciliation and the arts of peace, and reverence these glorious war-worn flags as mementoes of the power and will of the people—the glory of our arms, the saved and sacred honor of our country.

To you who tread the paths of politics and State, the faithful soldiers of the Republic, fresh from the field of victory and fame, now restore banners and bayonets, emblems of renown and glories won.

As you assume the weighty responsibilities shifted from the field to the forum, look at these and give us order and rest— look at these and be grateful that our country has passed through such an ordeal to come forth strong, vigorous and powerful, even as gold purified by fire.

To those who would urge you to think of commerce destroyed by foreign aid and comfort, furnished with the hope to overthrow our government, say to them that we are gainers if such acts give rules for our future guidance—or better, tell them that a free and powerful nation, conscious of its strength, wars not for pelf or passion, but for principle; that a generous appreciation of the honest hearts, whose sympathies were and ever are with peoples or nations that strive for freedom, effaces all recollection of the sordid, grasping wretches, that would trade even over the grave of liberty.

Do some, elated with our success, urge new wars? Tell them the terrible cost of war—say to them that did these emblems, wreathed with glory, speak only of valor and success in arms, as the lesson of the war, 'twould be too dearly bought; that above and beyond this they speak of man's capacity for greatest freedom. They speak of burdens assumed in every city, village and hamlet by our people. They tell the earnestness, the trials, the energy and devotion of patriotic men in civil power and life, who never faltered, never yielded, from duty's path, that self-government might be forever fixed.

This is no man's triumph, but a people's will, and a nation's fame. Unhallowed ambition gains nothing; honor rests only with those who have placed their country and the right before all else. The full measure of our success ends not with our ocean-bound limits. Freedom—prize of manhood's heart in every clime—breathes new life, gives renewed hope, and lives for all time.

This triumph gives to future ages a living monument, carved not in brass or stone, but perpetuated in the souls of all to whom are given mind's light—'Tis this—*God gives triumph only to the right.* Ever reading this in every living star and line of these glorious flags, let us be content with the results.

In the glorious future that lies before the country, redeemed and strengthened by trial, you will surely give to these banners an honored place in your halls—to those who return them to you, the warm welcome of love and recognition—to those who have fallen in their defense, tears of gratitude, with imperishable fame.

> "Oh, mothers, sisters, daughters, spare the tears ye fain would shed,
> Who seem to die in such a cause, ye cannot call them dead.
> They live upon the lips of men, in picture, bust and song,
> And nature folds them in her heart and keeps them safe from wrong."

RESPONDING ADDRESS,

BY GOVERNOR FENTON.

SADLY, yet proudly, I receive in behalf of the State these ensigns of our patriot soldiers — these emblems of a nation's life and manhood. These banners are eloquent evidences of the unwearied fidelity and unconquerable love of Union and Liberty of the soldiers of New York. They speak the silent yet impressive language of a nation's redemption and destiny. Under their folds our brothers pledged eternal devotion to country, and leaving the comforts and endearments of home, they went forth to assert the supremacy of the institutions the fathers had established, and to maintain them against treason's great conspiracy.

Tradition and the faithful chronicler of events will embalm the sublime truth, that the citizen soldier of the army of the Republic is the grandest embodiment of intelligence, patriotism and bravery the world has yet developed.

By them the great experiment of self-government has been settled for all people, in all countries beneath the sun. Our manhood has been elevated and strengthened, and liberty and popular institutions everywhere recognized as a permanent outgrowth of American destiny. We now enter upon a higher and nobler thought. We stand out from the common track of history — we rise above the best conditions of the past six thousand years, and write a new chapter in the social and political affairs of man.

All honor to the great general who led in triumph, to all the noble officers and men, by land and sea, who stood firm and uncomplaining amid the terrible strife, and thanks to the tried patriotism of the people who sustained, upheld and cheered them throughout the hard duties of the struggle. Forever let the memory of the heroes who fell remain with us. Forever remember with gratitude those who sacrificed, suffered or lost.

On this anniversary day — the day our fathers proclaimed the great truths upon which a nation laid its foundations — it is most proper we should assemble and redeclare our attachment to these principles, and our gratitude to the men who have not only sustained, but advanced, the standards of the Republic, and opened to us a new career of greater freedom.

Rarely has it occurred in the history of other nations, that the grand idea, the sublime purpose, which the Supreme Ruler of the affairs of men had steadily kept in view, has subdued the passions and inspired the thoughts of the combatants themselves.

Nearly every page of history has its records of strife, turmoil and bloodshed, often continuing for long periods, with little intermission, in which, for the time being, no great principle of humanity seems to be involved. Personal ambition, territorial aggrandizement, and religious fanaticism, have each in turn offered an excuse for the aggressions of power upon weakness.

People have fought blindly against present despotism, or nations as blindly for national existence, ennobled by no exalted idea of human rights, and encouraged by no abiding faith in the grand primal truth, that justice is born of God and must prevail. It is only when ages have passed, that the broadest intellects, aided by the philosophy of history, discover in this chaotic turmoil the purposes of Providence in the affairs of the human race.

How different the conflict in which this nation has been engaged! To each generation has been vouchsafed the seed-time and harvest of the principles it has sought to establish. The germ of religious and political freedom, planted at Plymouth Rock, extended slowly at first, but steadily overspread the whole land. In less than seven years from the enunciation of the sublime doctrine of civil rights, in the Declaration of Independence,—seven years of bloody war, in which a nation few in numbers, but strong in their cause, struggled with a powerful mother country,—and the success of every hope was attained. The seeds of civil liberty sown in strife and watered with blood, gave us the harvest which we have been reaping for eighty peaceful years. What a gathering of liberal sentiment it has been! What national prosperity has been ours! But if the elements of our strength grew rapidly under the auspices of the unparalleled freedom of our institutions, so likewise did the elements of weakness. You need no recital of events—no attempts at history. It is sufficient to say that while one half the nation turned all its energies to the acquisition of wealth, the other half sought for power. Each pursued its object with such steadiness of purpose and blind zeal, that in the end the North was banker for the South, and the South became the keeper of the Northern political consciences. The events of the day are familiar to you all. Then came this dreadful war. The wealth which the North had labored for with such eagerness, was poured out by the thousands of millions, and the noblest blood flowed like water, that we might regain the keeping of our consciences and the right to assert the dearest civil and political privileges. This is the great victory over which we rejoice to-day. The right to think and to act up to our highest conceptions of truth and justice. It is success in this cause which surrounds these frayed and tattered banners with a glory which no other victory could give; it ennobles the heroism of their brave defenders and gives crowns of martyrdom to those who fell beneath their shadow.

We will not, however, claim too much for ourselves. Let us acknowledge the goodness of God, whose providences are manifest in all our history. Let us not forget that the Puritans, themselves the apostles of religious freedom, were persecuted for righteousness' sake. The first blows of the Revolution were struck not solely for freedom, but against despotism. Four years ago the instincts of self-preservation marshaled our first armies against organized rebellion, not for the doctrine of human rights. But we were not compelled as other nations have been, to grope our way in darkness, blind to the purposes of the Almighty, till not only lives were lost, but whole generations had passed away and nationalities grown decrepid 'midst scenes of constant and unhopeful strife. Witness how in this last, the grandest struggle in our history, if not in all history, we were almost compelled to take the higher ground!

These banners, advanced in so just a cause as that of national unity and integrity, went forward seldom, faltered often, and were sometimes beaten back. Not until the divine right of freedom to all men was proclaimed, centering in them the hopes of manhood everywhere, and bringing to them the prayers of every Christian people, did they go forth in an almost uninterrupted course from victory to victory.

And now the noblest eulogy we can pronounce upon their brave defenders is, not merely that they have given release from strife, but they have uprooted the elements of civil discord—not that they have protected our rights only, but they have enfranchised a downtrodden race—not that they have preserved our ancient constitution only, but they have founded constitution and government anew in the principles of eternal justice.

These Flags are now deposited for permanent custody in the Bureau of Military Record.

HISTORY OF FLAGS.

COLORS OF THE 1st REGIMENT, N. Y. S. V.

Four Flags.)

1. *Regimental Banner*, silk; much worn. Presented to the Regiment by the City of New York.
2. *National Flag*, silk.
3, 4. *Guidons*.

The 1st Regiment was raised in the city of New York by WM. H. ALLEN. It was mustered into service April 22d, 1861; took part in the action at Big Bethel, June 10th, 1861; joined the army of the Potomac just subsequent to the battle at Fair Oaks (1862), and served with credit in the engagements at Peach Orchard, Glendale and Malvern Hill. At Glendale, out of four Sergeants, carrying the four Colors, and eleven Corporals, composing the Color-Guard, but one man escaped, the others being killed or wounded. On the 29th and 30th August, 1862, the Regiment took part in the second battle at Bull Run; on the 1st September, in the action at Chantilly; on the 13th, 14th and 15th December, in the attack on Fredericksburgh; and on the 1st, 2d, 3d, 4th and 5th of May, 1863, in the battles at Chancellorsville,—serving in the latter actions after the term of service of most of its members had expired.

These Flags were returned by Col. J. FREDERICK PIERSON, and were represented at the presentation by Capt. NORMAN B. LESLIE.

COLORS OF THE 2d REGIMENT, N. Y. S. V.

One Flag.

---

1. *National Flag*, silk; faded; with staff.

This Flag was received by the Regiment at Camp Hamilton, Va., in May, 1862. It was carried to Portsmouth, Fair Oaks and Harrison's Landing, and down the Peninsula to Yorktown, and in the battles and skirmishes before Richmond, from June 5th to August 20th, 1862. It was then taken to Alexandria and deposited with other property of the Regiment.

The 2d Regiment was recruited and organized in Troy, in April, 1861. It was the second Volunteer Regiment to leave the State, at the commencement of the war, and the first to encamp on the soil of Virginia. On the 10th of June, 1861, it took part in the first battle of the war at Big Bethel, Va. It was encamped at Camp Hamilton and Newport News during its first year's service. It joined the "Army of the Potomac," June 5th, 1862, and took part in the following engagements: Fair Oaks (June 21st and 25th), White Oak Swamp, Savage's Station, Centreville, Glendale, and Malvern Hill (June 30th and August 5th). It was subsequently in actions at Bristow Station, 2d Bull Run, Fredericksburgh, and Chancellorsville. During its period of service it lost only 15 killed and wounded, while it was reduced by deaths from disease, and absence on account of sickness, 163 men. It was mustered out May 26th, 1863.

COLORS OF THE 5th REGIMENT, N. Y. S. V.

Three Flags.

1. *National Flag*, silk. The streamers attached are embroidered as follows: "Fidéla á l'outrance," on the red. The staff is half cut in two by a shot. Presented to the Regiment by friends in New York city, through Capt. CAMBRELING. Was only in action at Big Bethel.

2. *National Flag*, silk. Inscription upon a silver plate on the staff: "Presented by the City of New York, 1862." Was in Peninsula campaign to Chancellorsville.

3. *Regimental Banner*, blue silk; arms and motto of the United States, and "Fifth Zouave Reg't, N. Y. V." painted; original staff, with top shot off in battle of Gaines' Mills. Received from General Government by Regiment.

The 5th Regiment was organized in the city of New York, under the auspices of Col. ABRAM DURYEE, in April, 1861, and was mustered into service May 9 of that year, for two years. It served in the following engagements, viz.: Little Bethel, Big Bethel, Siege of Yorktown as siege artillerists, Hanover Court House, Gaines' Mills, Charles City Cross Roads, Malvern Hill, Manassas Plains or 2d Bull Run, Antietam, Blackford Ford, Fredericksburgh, and Chancellorsville. At Gaines' Mills, Color-Sergeant ANDREW B. ALLISON bore the National Flag (No. 2), which was pierced by eight balls, one of which nearly severed the staff; and Color-Corporal LEON OLIVIA was killed. At 2d Bull Run, both Color-Sergeants and the entire Color-Guard were killed.

Represented at presentation by Lieutenant JOHN F. BURNS.

COLORS OF THE 6th REGIMENT, N. Y. S. V.

Four Flags.

---

1. *National Flag*, silk, with the following inscriptions: "Santa Rosa, Fort Pickens, Nov. 22 and 23, and Jan. 1, Pensacola, Irish Bend, Vermillion." On the staff is a silvered plate, with the inscription: "Presented to the 6th Regiment, Col. WILSON's Zouaves, by several ladies of New York city, June, 1861."

2. *Banner*, blue silk; presented by the City of New York, bearing upon each side the city arms, inscribed: "Fort Pickens, Nov. 22 and 23, Jan. 1, Santa Rosa, Pensacola, Irish Bend, and Vermillion."

3, 4. *Guidons*. Presented to the Regiment by T. C. BURNS, Esq., May 8, 1861.

The 6th Regiment was organized in the city of New York, by Col. WILLIAM WILSON, and was mustered in May 25, 1861, for two years. It was assigned to duty on Santa Rosa Island, Florida, where it rendered valuable service in the defense of Fort Pickens. In Nov., 1862, the Regiment went to New Orleans, and served with great credit in the Department of the Gulf. It returned to New York, June 10, 1863, with 506 of the 770 men who originally went out.

Represented at presentation by Lieut.-Colonel MICHAEL CASSIDY.

COLORS OF THE 8th REGIMENT, N. Y. S. V.

Three Flags.

---

1. *National Flag*, silk; staff gone.
2. *National Flag*, silk; original staff.
3. *Regimental Banner*, blue silk; painted arms of the city of New York. On plate, "8th Regiment, N. Y. S. V., 1863. Presented by the City of New York."

The 8th Regiment, or "1st German Rifles," was organized in the city of New York, under the first call of the President for volunteers (1861), and received about 800 men within 24 hours after its rolls were opened. It was mustered in on the 23d of April, 1861, and took the field (July 10th) in BLENKER'S Brigade, MILES' Division, of Gen. McDOWELL'S army. In the 1st Bull Run battle it was in the reserve under Col. MILES, and assisted materially in checking the advance of the enemy. In March, 1862, it was assigned to SUMNER'S Corps. In May, following, it was placed under Gen. FREMONT, in the Shenandoah valley,—was in the engagement at Cross Keys, where 260 of its men were left dead or wounded on the field. It was subsequently transferred to SIGEL'S Corps, and was in the action at Sulphur Springs, and the battle of 2d Bull Run. It arrived on the field too late to participate in the battle of Fredericksburgh, which was the last principal battle before the expiration of its term of enlistment.

COLORS OF THE 10th REGIMENT, N. Y. S. V.

Two Flags.

1. *National Flag*, silk; with staff. Presented to the Regiment, by Maj.-Gen. WOOL, at Fortress Monroe, Sept., 1861, on behalf of the city of New York.

This was the first American Flag raised over the Custom House at Norfolk, Va., after the recovery of that place by Union troops. It was borne in the Seven Days' Battles before Richmond, 2d Bull Run, Antietam, and Fredericksburgh. At the latter place it was shot from the hands of the bearer. Several of the guard were killed under it.

2. *Regimental Banner*, with staff and spear-head, the latter struck by a shot. Presented by Judge WHITE, of New York, on the departure of the Regiment for the seat of war.

At 2d Bull Run, the 5th and 10th N. Y. were sent into a piece of woods, and entirely flanked on both flanks by the enemy, and driven from the ground. The Color-Bearer of the 10th was killed, and the Flag here presented was captured by a Georgia Regiment and was taken to Milledgeville, where it was displayed in the capitol as a trophy. It was recaptured by Gen. SLOCUM's column of Gen. SHERMAN's army, on the march from Atlanta to Savannah. Col. RODGERS, of Gen. SLOCUM's staff, removed it from the capitol and transmitted it to the archives of the State, through Maj.-Gen. DANIEL BUTTERFIELD.

The 10th Regiment sprang from what was called the "Union Volunteers," of the city of New York, and was one of the first Regiments of volunteers offered to the Governor of this State, in 1861. It was organized under the command of Col. W. W. MCCHESNEY, and served in the following engagements, viz.: Big Bethel, Gaines' Mills, and Seven Days' Battles before Richmond, 2d Bull Run, South Mountain, Antietam, Shepardstown, and Fredericksburgh.

When the Regiment was mustered out, it left a battalion of four companies (since increased to six) in the field, under command of Maj. GEORGE F. HOPPER, which participated in the campaign of 1864–5.

COLORS OF THE 12th REGIMENT, N. Y. S. V.

One Flag.

---

1. *National Flag*, silk. Presented to the Regiment by the ladies of Syracuse, May 2d, 1861, and carried by the Regiment through every service in which it was engaged.

The 12th Regiment was organized at Syracuse in the spring of 1861. It was engaged in the battle of Blackburn's Ford, and at 1st Bull Run was in the reserve. After spending several months in building and guarding forts in front of Washington, it was sent to the Peninsula, and was subsequently engaged in the siege of Yorktown, and in the battles of Hanover Court House, Gaines' Mills, Savage's Station, White Oak Swamp, Malvern Hill, 2d Bull Run, and 1st Fredericksburgh. It returned to the State in the spring of 1863, at the expiration of its term of service.

Represented at presentation by Col. HENRY A. WEEKS.

COLORS OF THE 11th REGIMENT, N. Y. S. V.

Two Flags.

---

1. *National Flag*, silk; little worn; original staff. Presented by LAURA KEENE.

2. *Regimental Banner*, white silk; painted with arms of Fire Department of the city of New York; inscribed, "1st Regiment New York Zouaves"—"The Star Spangled Banner in triumph shall wave;" original staff, cord and tassels. Presented to the Regiment by JOHN R. PLATT, President, on behalf of the Fire Department of the city of New York.

The 11th Regiment, or "First Regiment New York Zouaves," was sometimes called the "First Fire Zouaves," and the "Ellsworth Zouaves." With the consent of President LINCOLN, Col. E. ELMER ELLSWORTH visited New York city, in April, 1861, and laid before the Chief of the Fire Department a proposition to raise a Regiment. With the concurrence of the Chief, offices were opened in each Fire District. This was on Friday. On Saturday 850 men were enrolled, and on Monday 1,300 men presented themselves. Eleven hundred and thirty men were selected, and were armed and equipped by the Fire Department. In the affair at the Marshall House, Col. ELLSWORTH was killed. After the battle of 1st Bull Run, the Regiment became demoralized and was disbanded in the spring of 1862.

The flag of the Marshall House, in removing which Col. ELLSWORTH was killed, has been deposited in connection with these Flags.

COLORS OF THE 13th REGIMENT, N. Y. S. V.

Three Flags.

---

1. *National Flag*, silk; with staff. This Flag was borne in the first battle of Bull Run only. The holes in its union were made upon that occasion.
2. *National Flag*, bunting; with staff. This Flag was carried by the Regiment in all its marches and actions.
3. *Regimental Banner*, blue silk; with staff; embroidered on one side with eagle and motto, "God and our country;" on the other, State arms painted, with number of Regiment. Presented to the Regiment by the ladies of Rochester.

The 13th Regiment was raised in Rochester, under Colonel (now General) ISAAC F. QUINBY, in April, 1861, and, with the 12th N. Y., was the first to pass through Baltimore after the riot of April 19th, and the attack upon the 6th Massachusetts. It participated in the first battle at Bull Run, siege of Yorktown, battles of Hanover Court House, Mechanicsville, Gaines' Mills, Turkey Bend, Malvern Hill, 2d Bull Run, Antietam (in reserve), Shepardstown and Fredericksburgh. After an honorable service of two years, the Regiment was mustered out, May 14, 1863.

COLORS OF THE 14th REGIMENT, N. Y. S. V.

One Flag.

---

1. *National Flag*, bunting; much worn; staff gone. Presented to the Regiment on its departure for the field, by Gov. MORGAN, on behalf of the State of New York, and returned to Gov. SEYMOUR, soiled and tattered, but not dishonored.

The 14th Regiment was organized at Albany, from companies raised in Utica, Rome, Boonville, Batavia, Lowville and Hudson. It joined the Army of the Potomac in June, 1861, and was engaged in the siege of Yorktown, and in the battles of New Bridge, Hanover Court House, Mechanicsville, Gaines' Mills, Malvern Hill, 2d Bull Run, Shepardstown, Fredericksburgh, and Chancellorsville. It has the proud record that it *never had its pickets driven in, and never turned its back to the enemy in battle.*

COLORS OF THE 16th REGIMENT, N. Y. S. V.

Two Flags.

---

1. *National Flag*, silk; faded and worn; with staff and spear-head. Presented to the Regiment by Mrs. Col. JOSEPH HOWLAND, at camp Franklin, near Alexandria, in March, 1862.

2. *Regimental Banner*, blue silk; painted with shield, &c., but almost entirely destroyed; staff, &c. Presented to the Regiment by Mrs. Col. JOSEPH HOWLAND, of Fishkill, N. Y., in June, 1861.

These Flags have been borne in eighteen battles, skirmishes and reconnoisances, the principal of which were West Point, Va., Gaines' Mills and the six following days of fighting and marching; Crampton Gap, Antietam, and 1st and 2d Fredericksburgh. At Gaines' Mills the Color-Bearers were three times shot down, and all except one of the Color-Guard were either killed or wounded. The Regimental Banner was in every march and in every battle in which the Regiment participated. It was struck by a ball, while in the hands of the Color-Bearer, and the ferule indented so that it could not be moved on the staff. At Crampton Gap, Corporal CHARLES H. CONANT was instantly killed by a Minie ball through the head, while holding one of the Flags, and Corporal ROBERT WATSON, of the Color-Guard, was shot through the leg. In this action, the Regiment, in charging upon the enemy, captured a rebel battle-flag from an Alabama Regiment.

The 16th Regiment was composed of companies raised in the counties of St. Lawrence, Clinton and Franklin. It left the State June 26, 1861. Upon the expiration of its term of two years, these Colors were presented to his Excellency, Gov. SEYMOUR—the pledge given by the Regiment to the donor, to "Stand by, defend and preserve them," having been faithfully and honorably redeemed.

COLORS OF THE 17th REGIMENT, N. Y. S. V.

Three Flags.

---

1. *National Flag*, silk; embroidered with number of Regiment; much worn; spear-head gone. Presented to the regiment by eight lady friends of Col. H. S. LANSING.

2. *Regimental Banner*, white silk; painted on one side with arms of State of New York, and "17th Regiment New York Volunteers," and on the other, with eagle, shield and number of Regiment. Original staff, with plate inscribed: "Presented to the Westchester Chasseurs by the ladies of Westchester county, May, 1861."

3. *Regimental Banner*, blue silk; painted with arms of the city of New York, and figures and words, "17th Reg. N. Y. V.; presented by the City of New York." Original staff gone.

The 17th Regiment, sometimes known as the "Westchester Chasseurs," was organized in the city of New York, in the spring of 1861. It was composed of four companies from Westchester county, one from Rockland, two from New York, one from Wayne, one from Wyoming, and one from Chenango. It left for the seat of war in June, 1861, and participated in the siege of Yorktown, and battles of Hanover Court House (where it captured the first cannon taken from the enemy by the army of the Potomac), Groveton (where it lost 13 officers and 250 men killed and wounded), Antietam, Fredericksburgh, and Chancellorsville. It was mustered out in the spring of 1863, after two years' service—was immediately reorganized for three years' service, and took the field in September, being the first of the thirty-nine old Regiments to report for duty.

COLORS OF THE 18th REGIMENT, N. Y. S. V.

One Flag.

---

1. *National Flag*, silk; with inscription: "Rally around them," "18th Reg. N. Y. V." Presented to the Regiment by the lady friends of Col. WILLIAM A. JACKSON, Albany, June 1, 1861, shortly before departure for the field.

The 18th Regiment was organized at Albany, from companies enlisted in Albany, Schenectady, Fishkill, Wallkill (Middletown), and Ogdensburgh. It was engaged in the battles of 1st Bull Run, West Point, Gaines' Mills (where it lost 180 men in killed, wounded, and missing), Charles City Cross Roads, Malvern Hill, Crampton Pass (where it took 100 prisoners and one battle-flag, and lost 58 men in killed, wounded, and missing), Antietam, 1st and 2d Fredericksburgh, and Chancellorsville. It lost but 15 men from sickness, but the casualties of war reduced its ranks to 425 men. It returned to the State, May 16, 1863, with a most honorable record of arduous and faithful service.

COLORS OF THE 21st REGIMENT, N. Y. S. V.

One Flag.

1. *National Flag*, silk; with staff.

This Flag was presented to the 21st Regiment by the young ladies of the Central School of the city of Buffalo, in the spring of 1861. It was carried by the Regiment in the following battles: Rappahannock Station, Sulphur Springs, Groveton, 2d Bull Run, Chantilly, South Mountain, Antietam, and Fredericksburgh. In the second battle at Bull Run, five enlisted men were killed and wounded while carrying it, and the eagle at the top of the staff was shot off.

The 21st, or "First Buffalo Regiment," was recruited in Buffalo, in the spring of 1861, under Col. WM. F. ROGERS. It was first attached to Gen. WADSWORTH's Brigade; subsequently joined the army under Gen. POPE as a part of McDOWELL's Corps; marched through Maryland, under Gen. HOOKER; and at Fredericksburgh formed part of REYNOLDS' Corps of FRANKLIN's Division. It lost 64 men killed and died of wounds, and had 173 wounded in battle. Its original strength was 780 officers and men, and it received about 150 recruits.

COLORS OF THE 22d REGIMENT, N. Y. S. V.

One Flag.

---

1. *National Flag*, silk; forty-six bullet holes in the Flag, and on the staff is a break where it was struck by a shot.

This was the second Flag carried by the Regiment, the first having been lost at 2d Bull Run, where the Regiment lost 266 men killed and wounded. It was carried in the battles of South Mountain, Fredericksburgh and Chancellorsville.

The 22d Regiment was principally from the counties of Warren, Essex and Clinton. It was organized at Troy, and mustered into service June 6, 1861. It took part in the battles of Gainesville, 2d Bull Run, South Mountain, Antietam, Rappahannock Station, Groveton, Fredericksburgh and Chancellorsville.

Represented at presentation by Capt. J. W. McCoy — carried by Private John White.

COLORS OF THE 24th REGIMENT, N. Y. S. V.

One Flag.

---

1. *National Flag*, silk, with original staff.

This Flag is inscribed with its own history. Upon one side, "Falmouth, Rappahannock Station, Warrenton Springs, Gainesville, Groveton, 2d Bull Run, South Mountain, Antietam, Fredericksburgh, Rappahannock Crossing, Chancellorsville," and upon the other, "24th Regiment, Iron Brigade, 1st Division, 1st Army Corps."

This Regiment was mostly enlisted in the county of Oswego. It was organized at Oswego; entered the field in 1861, and served during the active campaign of 1862. It was mustered out in the spring of 1863, after participating in the battle of Chancellorsville.

COLORS OF THE 25th REGIMENT, N. Y. S. V.

One Flag.

---

1. *National Flag*, silk; much worn and torn; no staff.

The 25th Regiment was organized in the city of New York, under the auspices of Colonel JAMES E. KERRIGAN, and was mustered into the service of the United States June 26, 1861. It was in the extreme advance at Yorktown, April 5, 1862; took a prominent part in the action at Hanover, May 27, and in the Seven Days' Battles before Richmond. It was also engaged at 2d Bull Run, Antietam, Shepardstown, Fredericksburgh and Chancellorsville.

This Flag was borne with honor in the engagements named.

COLORS OF THE 26th REGIMENT, N. Y. S. V.

One Flag.

---

1. *National Flag*, bunting.

This Flag was carried by the Regiment during its entire term of service. It bears the marks of bullets and of blood. Five good and true men having fallen beneath its folds.

The 26th Regiment was raised by Col. WM. H. CHRISTIAN. It was organized at Elmira from companies recruited in Utica, Hamilton, and Rochester, and in Tioga county. It served under Gen. POPE, in Virginia; under Gen. McCLELLAN, in Maryland; under Gen. BURNSIDE, at Fredericksburgh; and under Gen. HOOKER, at Chancellorsville. It was in the battles of Cedar Mountain, Rappahannock Station, Thoroughfare Gap, Groveton, South Mountain, Antietam, Fredericksburgh, and Chancellorsville. At Groveton, about 150 were killed and wounded; at Antietam, 30; and at Fredericksburgh, 162.

Represented at presentation by Lieut.-Col. G. S. JENNINGS.

COLORS OF THE 27th REGIMENT, N. Y. S. V.

Two Flags.

---

1. *National Flag*, silk; much worn.

The 27th Regiment received this Flag, May 22d, 1861, from Company G, and this company received it the same day from Mrs. PHILIP CHURCH, of Belvidere. It was borne in the battles of 1st Bull Run, Mechanicsville, West Point, Gaines' Mills, Goldsborough's Farm, Chickahominy, White Oak Creek, Malvern Hill, Crampton Pass, Antietam, and the 1st and 2d battles of Fredericksburgh. The bearer at Gaines' Mills was severely wounded. The Flag has been many times struck by the enemy's shot, and the larger holes were made by fragments of shell. The star, in the case appended to the lance, was literally shot out of the Flag while the Regiment was storming the Heights of Fredericksburgh, in May, 1863. It was contributed by A. L. VAN NESS, of Dansville, N. Y., who was the Color-Bearer in that assault.

2. *National Flag*, silk.

This Flag was presented to Company H, May 16th, 1861, by the ladies of Mount Morris, Livingston Co.; was returned by the Company to the donors, May 21st, 1863, and by the latter deposited in the State archives.

The 27th Regiment was organized at Elmira from companies raised in Rochester, Binghamton, Lyons, Angelica, and Lima, and entered the field under Col. SLOCUM, since promoted to the rank of Major-General. Col. BARTLETT, who succeeded, was promoted to the command of a division.

COLORS OF THE 28th REGIMENT, N. Y. S. V.

One Flag.

---

1. *Guidon,* silk.

At the battle of Chancellorsville, JOHN OTTO SWAN, of Medina, aged fifteen years (enlisted as a drummer, and then acting as a marker), displayed great activity and energy. A soldier of Company E was shot dead, when the boy took this Flag from its staff, put it in his pocket, adjusted upon himself the accoutrements of the dead soldier, and fought gallantly in the ranks until, with sixty-five men and three officers, he was taken prisoner. Concealing the Flag under the lining of his coat, he kept it with him when taken to Richmond, and managed to bring it away unobserved when exchanged and sent home. The Flag has been deposited by the lad's father, as an honorable memorial of the services of a patriotic son.

The 28th Regiment was organized at Albany, May 18, 1861, from companies recruited at Lockport, Medina, Canandaigua, Batavia, Albion, Niagara Falls, and Monticello. Its first service was under Gen. PATTERSON, at Martinsburg, Va., where Co. A lost one man killed. Afterwards, in the campaign under Gen. BANKS, it was under fire not less than twenty times, and was in the actions at Point of Rocks, 1st and 2d Winchester, and Cedar Mountain. In the latter engagement the Regiment distinguished itself, and suffered heavily, having lost 207 in killed, wounded and prisoners, including among the killed the brave and lamented Col. DUDLEY DONNELLY. The Colors of the Regiment were lost in this engagement, after being nobly and gallantly defended in a hand to hand conflict with greatly superior numbers. Eleven bullet holes had been made in it, its staff shot nearly off, and three of its bearers mortally wounded, when it was taken by the enemy. In the battle at Antietam the Regiment won a tribute to its valor, and it continued to render honorable service until the expiration of its term of two years.

COLORS OF THE 29th REGIMENT, N. Y. S. V.

Three Flags and Two Guidons.

1. *National Flag*, silk; much worn and tattered; the service Flag of the Regiment. Presented by the City of New York.

2. *National Flag*, silk; in good condition; plate on staff inscribed, "29th Regiment, N. Y. Vols., 1863. Presented by the City of New York."

3. *Regimental Banner*, blue silk; painted arms of the city of New York, and inscription, "29th Regiment, N. Y. V. Presented by the City of New York."

4, 5. *Guidons*, silk.

Thirty-three men were killed while fighting under these colors.

The 29th Regiment was composed exclusively of Germans, and was organized in the city of New York under Col. (now General) A. VON STEINWEHR. It was engaged in the battles of 1st Bull Run, Cross Keys, Warrenton, Sulphur Springs, 2d Bull Run, and Chancellorsville. It was a part of the 1st Brigade, 2d Division, 11th Army Corps, and during the active period of the campaign of 1862, served under Gen. FREMONT, in the Mountain Department, and in the corps of Gen. SIGEL, in the army of Virginia. It went to the field with 745 men, and returned with 339, at the expiration of its term of two years.

COLORS OF THE 30th REGIMENT, N. Y. S. V.

One Flag.

1. *National Flag*, bunting; original staff gone.

At the second battle of Bull Run, these Colors fell, during the engagement, in the hands of ten different men shot dead on the field. Thirty-six balls passed through the Stars and Stripes, and the staff was shot into splinters. Two hundred men, out of three hundred and forty-one, were killed or wounded; fourteen, out of seventeen line officers fell upon the field, among whom was Col. EDWARD FRISBY, of Albany.

The 30th Regiment was raised in the counties of Washington, Albany, Rensselaer, Saratoga, Warren, Columbia, and Dutchess. It participated in the battles of Falmouth, Rappahannock Crossing, Gainesville, Groveton, Bull Run (2d), South Mountain, Antietam, and Fredericksburgh. At the battle of Antietam only forty-nine officers and men reported for duty. At the battle of South Mountain it captured three stands of colors from the enemy, and at Antietam four of the enemy's Flags rewarded its valor. It left for the field with 800 men, which number was increased to 1,050 by recruits. In January, 1863, only 397 men reported for duty, making a loss to the Regiment, in killed, wounded, discharged and absent, of 653.

Represented at presentation by Surgeon F. L. R. CHAPIN.

COLORS OF THE 32d REGIMENT, N. Y. S. V.

Two Flags.

---

1. *National Flag*, silk; with staff. Plate on staff engraved; "Presented to the 32d Regt., N. Y. S. Vols., June 28th, 1861, by Mrs. WM. LAIMBIER, Jr."
2. *Regimental Banner*, blue silk; painted with arms of the city of New York, inscribed, "32d Regiment, N. Y. V. Presented by the City of New York." Original staff, cord and tassels. About one-half of Banner gone.

The National Flag was presented to the Regiment, June 28, 1861, by the lady of the Hon. WM. LAIMBIER, Jr., of New York city; and the Banner by the city of New York in the fall of 1861. These Flags have been borne with honor in seven battles.

The 32d Regiment was originally intended to serve under Col. BAKER, of California, and for a time was called the "1st California Regiment." It was organized on Staten Island from companies enlisted in Johnstown, Amsterdam, Ithaca, Tarrytown, and New York city. It was engaged in the first battle of Bull Run, West Point, Gaines' Mills, White Oak Swamp, Charles City Cross Roads, 2d Bull Run, Crampton Pass, Antietam, Fredericksburgh, and Chancellorsville. During its two years' term of service, the Regiment lost 34 killed, and 127 wounded, in action. Its Colonel, RODERICK MATHESON, and its Major, CHARLES HUBBS, were mortally wounded at Crampton Pass, where the Regiment charged the enemy, and assisted in driving them up and over the mountain, with heavy loss.

COLORS OF THE 34th REGIMENT, N. Y. S. V.

One Flag.

1. *National Flag*, bunting; staff gone.

The 34th Regiment was organized at Albany in May, 1861. Five of its companies were enrolled in Herkimer county, two in Steuben, one in Clinton, one in Essex, and one in West Troy (Albany county). It was mustered into the service of the United States June 15th, and, soon after being sent to the seat of war, was assigned to duty in Maryland, on the Upper Potomac. It participated in seventeen battles, and in numerous skirmishes; among the former, Ball's Bluff, Siege of Yorktown, West Point, Fair Oaks, Seven Pines, Peach Orchard Station, Savage's Station, White Oak Swamp, Glendale, Malvern Hill, South Mountain, Antietam, Ashby's Gap, and Fredericksburgh. It never failed in duty to its country or in devotion to its Flag.

COLORS OF THE 35th REGIMENT, N. Y. S. V.

Two Flags.

---

1. *Regimental Banner*, silk; richly embroidered with the State arms and motto, and inscribed, "Jefferson Co., 35th Regiment, N. Y. S. V." "The Union, the Constitution, and the Enforcement of the Laws."
2. *National Flag*, silk; worn.

The Regimental Banner was obtained by subscription on the part of the officers of the Regiment. The National Flag was purchased by Hons. A. W. CLARK and C. B. HOARD and others. They were borne by the Regiment in the following engagements: Rappahannock, White Sulphur Springs, Groveton, 2d Bull Run, Chantilly, South Mountain, Antietam, and Fredericksburgh.

Six companies of the 35th Regiment were from Jefferson county, one from Lewis, one from Madison, one from Chemung and Steuben, and one from New York, Erie county and Elmira. It was mustered into service July 7, 1861, was placed under the command of Brig.-Gen. McDOWELL, and served under Brig.-Gen. JAMES S. WADSWORTH, from September, 1861, to March, 1862.

COLORS OF THE 37th REGIMENT, N. Y. S. V.

Six Flags.

---

1. *National Flag*, bunting; with original staff. Presented to the Regiment in July, 1861.

In camp or bivouac, this Flag was always placed on the color-line in front of the Colonel's tent. It was in the following battles, viz.: 1st Bull Run (in reserve), Williamsburgh, Fair Oaks, Glendale, Malvern Hill, 2d Bull Run, Chantilly, Fredericksburgh, and Chancellorsville, and in several skirmishes before Yorktown and Richmond in 1862.

2. *Brigade Battle-Flag* (red, white and red), bunting, with the number (1) in the centre to designate both the Brigade and the ranking Regiment of the Brigade. Received at Hampton, Va., April, 1862.

This Flag was also placed in front of the Colonel's quarters. It was in the battles already named except 1st Bull Run.

3. *National Flag*, silk.

The Regiment received a new stand of colors from the city of New York, in February, 1863, comprising a National Flag, Regimental Banner, and two Guidons. The National Flag belonging to this stand was lost at Chancellorsville during the murderous midnight engagement between the Third Corps and STONEWALL JACKSON'S division, in which JACKSON received his death wound. It was removed from the staff by LLOYD, the bearer, and wrapped around his body, as it was liable to be torn in passing the tangled brush through which he was obliged to creep. This brave and intelligent soldier was killed, and his body was buried without suspecting that the Flag was wrapped around his person, under his coat. Repeated efforts were made to find his grave, but without success. This Flag replaced the original.

4. *Regimental Banner*, green silk; emblazoned with Harp and Shamrock, and the inscriptions: "37th Regiment Irish Rifles, N. Y. Volunteers." "The first Regiment of Irish volunteers in the field." "Williamsburgh," "Fair Oaks," "Glendale," "Malvern Hill," "Fredericksburgh." Presented to the regiment by the City of New York, February, 1863.

This Banner was with the Regiment at Chancellorsville.

5, 6. *Guidons*, blue silk. Presented to the Regiment by the City of New York, February, 1863.

The 37th Regiment was raised in the city of New York, and, as already stated, was the first Regiment of Irish volunteers in the field. It was mustered out in 1863, after an honorable service of two years.

COLORS OF THE 38th REGIMENT, N. Y. S. V.

Two Flags.

---

1. *National Flag*, bunting.
2. *Regimental Banner*, blue silk; emblazoned with arms of the city of New York and "38th Regiment, N. Y. Volunteers. Presented by the City of New York."

These colors were presented to the Regiment by the citizens and the city of New York. They were not received by the Regiment until after its engagement in the battle of 1st Bull Run, but were borne in all its subsequent services.

The 38th Regiment was organized in the city of New York in the spring of 1861, and was known as the "Second Regiment Scott Life Guard." It was composed of seven companies from New York city, one company from Horseheads, one from Geneva, and one from Elizabethtown. It participated in the first battle of Bull Run, in the siege of Yorktown, and in the battles of Williamsburgh, Fair Oaks, The Orchard, Charles City Cross Roads, Malvern Hill, 2d Bull Run, Chantilly, Fredericksburgh, Chancellorsville, and Gettysburg. It left New York with 829 men, and returned with 279, and during its term of service traveled nine hundred and ninety-seven miles, principally in the State of Virginia.

COLORS OF THE 40th REGIMENT, N. Y. S. V.

One Flag.

1. *National Flag*, bunting; much worn; original staff.

This Flag was presented to the Regiment, July 3d, 1861, at Yonkers, N. Y., by Hon. Fernando Wood, Mayor of New York, on behalf of the Union Defense Committee. It was borne in the sieges of Yorktown and Richmond (1862), and in the battles of Williamsburgh, Fair Oaks, Robinson's Field, Glendale, White Oak Swamp, Malvern Hill, Hay Market, Bull Run (2d), and Chantilly, besides several skirmishes. Color-Sergeant JOSEPH CONROY carried this Flag into action at Fair Oaks, and was killed on that field. Color-Corporal CHAS. BOYLE then took the colors; was wounded and ordered to the rear; refused to go, and was killed soon after. Color-Corporal GEO. MILLER bore it at Robinson's Field, Glendale, Malvern Hill, Hay Market, Bull Run and Chantilly. He died of disease. Color-Corporal ALFRED CONKLIN carried it at Williamsburgh, Fair Oaks and Malvern Hill. He died of disease at Harrison's Landing. Color-Corporal EDWIN HOWARD carried it at Bull Run and Chantilly; was distinguished in all the battles of the regiment, and wounded at Fredericksburgh. Color-Corporal OLIVER P. BISBING carried it at Williamsburgh and Fair Oaks, and was killed in the last named battle. Color-Corporal JOHN BRUNDAGE carried it at Williamsburgh, Fair Oaks, Glendale,

Malvern Hill and Bull Run, and was killed in the latter battle. Private JOSEPH BROWNE carried it at Hay Market, Bull Run, and Chantilly; was distinguished in eight engagements, and was promoted Color-Sergeant. Color-Corporal ROBERT GRIEVES carried it at Williamsburgh, Fair Oaks and Malvern Hill; was wounded and promoted at Fair Oaks. Color-Corporal THOS. READ carried it at Williamsburgh, Fair Oaks, Malvern Hill, Bull Run and Chantilly; was always distinguished, and was afterwards killed at Fredericksburgh. Color-Corporal THOS. BRASLIN carried it at Fair Oaks, and was dangerously wounded. Color-Corporal HORATIO N. SHEPHERD carried it at Malvern Hill, Bull Run and Chantilly. Color-Corporal JACOB D. BENNETT carried it at Williamsburgh. Color-Corporal WILLIAM MOYNE carried it at Williamsburgh, Fair Oaks and Malvern Hill; and Color-Corporal JOEL SLATTERY carried it at Malvern Hill, Bull Run and Chantilly; was afterwards badly wounded at Fredericksburgh. Whatever may have been the fortunes of the field, in the face of the enemy, the course of this Flag, in the hands of the Color-Guard named, was always *forward*.

The 40th Regiment was organized in the city of New York in April, 1861, under the synonym "Constitution Guard." It was accepted by the Union Defense Committee, and its name changed to "Mozart Regiment." It left for the seat of war, July 4, 1861, with about 1,000 men, splendidly armed and equipped, with two pieces of artillery, &c. It subsequently absorbed, by consolidation, the 55th, 87th and 101st Regiments, and the three years men of the 37th and 38th. It was one of the fighting Regiments of the war; bears on its record, Williamsburgh, Fair Oaks, Seven Days' Battles, Bull Run (2d), Chantilly, Fredericksburgh, Chancellorsville,

Gettysburg, Auburn, Orange Grove and Kelly's Ford; was honorably mentioned by MCCLELLAN, HEINTZELMAN, PORTER, KEARNEY, SEDGWICK, POPE, BURNSIDE, BIRNEY, BERRY, HOOKER and WARD, and sealed its devotion to the nation, whose emblem it carried, by the loss of 936 men in battle.

COLORS OF THE 43d REGIMENT, N. Y. S. V.

One Flag.

---

1. *National Flag*, bunting.

This Flag was obtained from the general government, and was carried by the Regiment until about the middle of September, 1862, when it gave place to a silk Flag presented by the ladies of the city of New York. The new Flag was carried until the 6th of May, 1864, when, with its bearer, Sergeant HACKETT, it was captured by the enemy. Sergeant HACKETT concealed the colors on his person, and, after his death in Andersonville prison, they were buried with his body. In July, 1864, the Regiment was presented, by the Albany Burgesses Corps, with a Flag and Guidons, which were carried until the close of the war.

The 43d Regiment was recruited in the counties of Albany, Montgomery, Washington and Otsego, and in New York city. It left Albany September 16, 1861, under command of Colonel (afterwards Brig.-Gen.) FRANCIS L. VINTON; arrived in the field September 21, 1861, and from that time until it was mustered out was constantly in the face of the enemy, skirmishing, reconnoitering and taking part in all the great events of the war. It went out with 706 men, and with the recruits which it subsequently received (including five companies recruited for it at the close of the Peninsula campaign in 1862), had a roll of 2,327. It returned with 291 men and

13 officers. It was first assigned to Gen. HANCOCK's Brigade, in which it served until February, 1863, when it was selected as one of five Regiments, distinguished for dash and courage, to form a Light Division in the Sixth Army Corps. It served in this division at Marye's Heights, Salem Church and Banks' Ford, and was the first Regiment that planted its colors on the enemy's works on Marye's Heights. After the Chancellorsville campaign, the Light Division was discontinued, and the Regiment was assigned to the 3d Brigade, 2d Division, Sixth Corps, in which it subsequently served. It was mustered out June 27, 1865, with the following battles, actions and sieges inscribed on its banners: Lee's Mills, April 29, 1862; Warwick Creek, April 30, 1862; Siege of Yorktown, 1862; Golding's Farm, June 27, 1862; Seven Days' Battles, 1862; Antietam, September 17, 1862; Fredericksburgh, December 12, 13, 14, 1862; Marye's Heights, May 3, 1863; Salem Church, May 3, 4, 1863; Banks' Ford, May 4, 1863; Fredericksburgh, June 5, 1863; Gettysburg, July 2, 3, 1863; Rappahannock Station, November 7, 1863; Locust Grove, November 27, 1863; Mine Run, November 29, 1863; Wilderness, May 5, 6, 1864; Spottsylvania, May 10, 12, 18, 1864; North Anna, May 23, 1864; Coal Harbor, June 1, 2, 3, 1864; Petersburgh, June 18, 28, 1864; Fort Stevens, D. C., July 12, 1864; Charlestown, August 21, 1864; Opequan, September 19, 1864; Fisher's Hill, September 22, 1864; Cedar Creek, October 19, 1864; Petersburgh, March 25, 1865; Petersburgh, April 2, 1865; Sailor's Creek, April 6, 1865; Surrender of LEE, April 9, 1865.

COLORS OF THE 44th REGIMENT, N. Y. S. V.

Two Flags.

---

1. *National Flag*, silk; faded, and ragged; letters and words in gilt, "P. E. R. 44th Reg. N. Y. V." The following inscription is engraved on the plate attached to the staff: "Presented by Mrs. ERASTUS CORNING, Albany, Oct. 21, 1861; returned to the donor, Jan., 1863, in exchange for a new Flag, and by her deposited in the Bureau of Military Statistics."

This Flag was borne by the Regiment in all its engagements up to January, 1863, viz.: Siege of Yorktown, Hanover Court House,* Gaines' Mills, Turkey Island Bend, Malvern Hill, 2d Bull Run, Antietam (in reserve), Shepardstown Ford, and Fredericksburgh.

2. *National Flag*, silk; much worn. Presented by Mrs. ERASTUS CORNING, January, 1863, in exchange for the orignal Flag of the Regiment, and deposited by her in the Bureau.

This Flag was carried by the Regiment in all its engagements during the years 1863 and 1864, and was brought home by it in October of the latter year. In the action at Spottsylvania Court House, about eighteen inches of the staff was taken off, and also the eagle and top of staff, by shot.

---

* At the battle of Hanover Court House, May 27, 1862, Corporal JAMES YOUNG, of Co. F, twice raised the fallen Flag of the Regiment, which had been shot down by the terrible cross-fire which swept the field. He fell pierced by a rifle-ball in the head, while waving his hat and shouting defiance to the enemy.

The 44th Regiment was organized by the *Ellsworth Association* in the fall of 1861, and was composed of representatives from different towns, villages and cities. It was mustered into service September 24, 1861, and served in the following engagements, viz.: Siege of Yorktown, Hanover Court House, Gaines' Mills, Turkey Island Bend, Malvern Hill, 2d Bull Run or Groveton, Antietam, Fredericksburgh, Chancellorsville, Aldie, Gettysburg, Jones' Cross Roads, Rappahannock Station, Mine Run, Wilderness, Spottsylvania Court House, North Anna, Bethesda Church, and through the series of battles and skirmishes before Petersburgh and on the Weldon railroad, up to September 24, 1864.

The heroic Gen. RICE, who was killed in the battle of the Wilderness, went out as Lieut.-Colonel of this Regiment, and Gen. CHAPIN, who was killed at Port Hudson was its original senior Captain.

COLORS OF THE 46th REGIMENT, N. Y. S. V.

Three Flags.

---

1. *National Flag*, silk; bears the following inscription on the staff: "Presented to the 46th Regiment, N. Y. S. V., VIELE's Brigade, by Mrs. E. L. VIELE, of the Union Defense Committee, New York, through their Commander, Colonel RUDOLPH ROSA, Oct. 12, 1861."

2. *Regimental Banner*, silk; with arms of the city of New York painted upon each side. Presented by the City of New York.

3. *National Flag*, silk; much worn. The streamers bear the following inscriptions: "Antietam, Md.; Fredericksburgh, Va.; East Tennessee; 2d Bull Run; Chantilly, Va.; South Mountain, Md.; Port Royal, S. C.; Pulaski, Ga.; James Island, S. C." Presented by the ladies of Washington, D. C., while the Regiment was encamped at Annapolis.

The 46th Regiment was organized in New York city, by Col. RUDOLPH ROSA, and left the State September 16, 1861. It was in the Port Royal expedition, in November, 1861; served in the siege of Fort Pulaski; was transferred from the Department of the South, July, 1862, to the army under Gen. POPE; was in engagements, viz.: Silver Spring, 2d Bull Run, Chantilly, Fairfax Court House, South Mountain, Antietam, and Fredericksburgh; from thence transferred to Kentucky, and served under Gen. GRANT at Vicksburg; from thence to Gen. BURNSIDE's command, in the operations around Knoxville, until date of re-enlistment and muster out.

At Jackson, Miss., the Regiment captured a large Texas flag; red, white and blue bars, and large white star in field, which has also been deposited in the archives of the State.

Represented on presentation by Col. G. W. TRAVERS.

COLORS OF THE 48th REGIMENT, N. Y. S. V.

One Flag.

---

1. *National Flag*, silk; completely riddled; part of original staff.

This Flag was presented to the Regiment by Mrs. Gen. VIELE, October, 1861, at Annapolis, Md. It was in a shower of bullets for three hours, and completely riddled. Part of the staff was shot away at Fort Wagner. It was borne in action at Port Royal Ferry (Jan. 1, 1862), Pocataligo (Oct. 22, 1862), Morris Island (July 10, 1863), and Fort Wagner (July 18, 1863). Of its bearers, Sergeant GEORGE G. SPARKS was wounded and transferred to Invalid Corps; Corporal GEORGE VREDENBERG was wounded and discharged; Corporal JAMES W. DUNN was wounded, promoted Captain, and killed at Fort Fisher; Corporal ALONZO HILLIKER was killed; Corporal ALEXANDER HYERS was killed, and Corporal SIDNEY WADHAMS was killed.

The 48th was Col. PERRY's Regiment, the "Continental Guard." It was organized in Brooklyn, and embraced volunteers recruited in that city and in New York, in Monmouth, N. J., and in towns and villages along Hudson's river, the Erie railroad, &c. It left the State Sept. 17, 1861, and was first assigned to VIELE's Brigade. It was present at the taking of Hilton Head; took part in the battle of Port Royal Ferry; built batteries on the Savannah river for the reduction of

Fort Pulaski; was in battle at Pocataligo, and captured one of the colors of the enemy; made several raids during the winter of 1863–4, and destroyed extensive salt works, &c.; formed part of the assaulting force on Morris Island, where it lost 53 in killed and wounded; and in the assault on Fort Wagner, where it lost 13 officers and 230 men in killed and wounded; in the battle of Olustee, where it lost 2 officers and 212 men in killed and wounded; joined the Army of the James in May, 1864, and was in the following engagements, viz.: Chester Hill (lost 39 men), Drury's Bluff (lost 3 officers and 76 men), Coal Harbor (lost 6 officers and 75 men), Petersburgh (lost 1 officer and 20 men), Mine Explosion (lost 2 officers and 27 men), Aug. 14th (lost 1 officer and 3 men), Aug. 16th (lost 4 officers and 50 men), Chapin's Farm (lost 1 officer and 2 men), Fort Fisher (lost 3 officers and 11 men), Wilmington (lost 1 officer and 15 men). It took the field with 910 men, and received 1,008 recruits. In the winter of 1864–5, 350 men reënlisted as veteran volunteers.

COLORS OF THE 49th REGIMENT, N. Y. S. V.

Two Flags.

1. *National Flag*, bunting; staff gone.

This Flag was presented to the 49th Regiment by Gov. MORGAN, on behalf of the State of New York, in Sept., 1861. It was used for a few months (in skirmish at Lewinsville, Oct. 14, 1861), until the presentation of a silk Banner to the Regiment, by the ladies of Buffalo, in the spring of 1862, when it was laid aside. In Sept., 1864, the original officers and privates (98 in number), were mustered out and took the silk color with them. The reënlisted veterans and the recruits were then organized as a Battalion, and a pole was cut and the old bunting again raised. Two days after, it was in the battle of Opequan (Sept. 19), at Fisher's Hill (Sept. 21, 22), and at Cedar Creek (Oct. 19). In December the Battalion returned with the Corps (Sixth) to Petersburgh, was engaged (March 25th and 27th) at Fort Fisher, near Petersburgh; formed the center of the assaulting column on the 2d of April, and planted this Flag, "the first Union color on the South Side Road." The Battalion followed Gen. LEE to Clover Hill, then returned to Burkesville Junction, where this Flag was replaced by a new Regimental Banner. Eighty-five officers and men were killed or wounded under this Flag, including Col. E. D. HOLT, who was wounded April 2d and died the 7th.

HISTORY OF FLAGS.

2. *National Flag*, silk; worn; original staff with plate inscribed with names of presentors—Mrs. ABBEY P. HEACOCK, Hon. WM. G. FARGO, and eighteen others.

This was the battle-flag of the Regiment from the spring of 1862 until October, 1864, when the Regiment was mustered out. It was borne in the following engagements, viz.: Watt's Creek, Young's Mills, Wyndi Mills, Siege of Yorktown, Mechanicsville, Garnett's Farm, Golden's Farm, Savage's Station, White Oak Swamp, Malvern Hill, 2d Bull Run, South Mountain, Antietam, 1st Fredericksburgh, Marye's Heights, Salem Heights, Skirmishes of June 5th and 6th, Gettysburg, Fairfield, Funckstown, Rappahannock Station, Mine Run, Wilderness (two), Spottsylvania, North Anna, Coal Harbor, Petersburgh, Gurley's House, Fort Stevens (Washington), Charlestown and Opequan Creek.

The 49th Regiment was organized at Buffalo, in the fall of 1861, under the command of Col. (afterwards Brig.-Gen.) D. D. BIDWELL. Companies B, D, E, and F, were raised in Erie Co.; Co's A, G, I, and K, in Chautauqua Co.; Co. C in Westchester, and Co. H. in Niagara. It was brigaded in 3d Brigade, of SMITH's Division, afterwards 2d Division of Sixth Army Corps. It was with the Army of the Potomac until July 9th, 1864, when it went with the Sixth Corps to the defense of Washington, and to the field under SHERIDAN. Its services are stated in the history of its Flags.

COLORS OF THE 57th REGIMENT, N. Y. S. V.

One Flag.

---

1. *National Flag*, silk; faded; half gone; rent by bullets and shell.

The 57th Regiment was organized in the city of New York in the fall of 1861, and left for Washington Nov. 28th of that year. During the year 1862 it was engaged in the following actions, viz.: Cedar Run, Fair Oaks, Gaines' Mills, Savage's Station, Peach Orchard, Glendale, Malvern Hill, Antietam and Fredericksburgh, and in subsequent active service.

COLORS OF THE 59th REGIMENT N. Y. S. V.

Ten Flags.

---

1. *National Flag*, silk; much worn; original staff gone. Presented to the Regiment by ex-Mayor KINGSLAND on behalf of the city of New York, Oct., 1861.
2. *National Flag*, silk; worn and faded; original staff.
3. *National Flag*, silk; worn; original staff. Presented to the Regiment by the City of New York, April, 1863.
4. *Regimental Banner*, blue silk, emblazoned with arms of the city of New York, number of Regiment, &c. Presented to the Regiment by the City of New York, Oct., 1863.
5, 6. *Guidons* (two), blue silk, emblazoned with arms of the State of New York. Presented to the Regiment by the City of New York, April, 1863.
7. *National Flag*, silk; original staff.
8. *Regimental Banner*, blue silk, emblazoned with arms of the State of New York; original staff.
9, 10. *Guidons* (two), bunting; original staff.

The 59th Regiment has returned three series of Flags. Flags 1 and 2 were carried in all the battles and skirmishes in which the Regiment participated, up to and including Gettysburg (July 3, 1863), where seven of the eight Color-Corporals were either killed or wounded. Out of twenty-one officers and three hundred and sixty men, thirteen officers and two hundred and thirty men were killed, wounded or taken prisoners at Antietam.

In the charge on Marye's Heights, a shell from the enemy

exploded directly over the second series of colors, shattered the top of the staff of the Regimental Banner, and tore both Flags (3 and 4) into shreds. The Guidons were only used on dress parades and drills.

The Flags of the third series were presented to the Regiment by Col. WM. A. OLMSTED, November, 1864. They have not been much worn, although marked by bullets received in the siege of Petersburgh, and in the numerous engagements which eventuated in the surrender of Gen. LEE.

The 59th was originally a mixed Regiment, composed in part of recruits enlisted in New York city, in Jefferson, Lewis, Putnam and Westchester counties, and in Ohio. It was organized in the city of New York in October, 1861, and left the State in November of that year. It reënlisted as a veteran command in the spring of 1864. By General Orders, the Regiment is entitled to have the following named battles inscribed on its Colors and Guidons, viz.: Blackburn's Ford, 1st Bull Run, Ball's Bluff, Yorktown, West Point, Fair Oaks, Peach Orchard, Savage's Station, Nelson's Farm, White Oak Swamp, Glendale, Malvern Hill, 2d Bull Run, South Mountain, Antietam, Fredericksburgh, Chancellorsville, Gettysburg, Bristow Station, Mine Run, Morton's Ford, Wilderness, Spottsylvania, Po River, North Anna, Coal Harbor, Petersburgh, Strawberry Plains, Deep Bottom, Reams' Station, Jerusalem Plank Road, Hatcher's Run, Armstrong's Mills, Dabney's Mills, Amelia Court House, High Bridge, Farmville, Surrender of LEE and his army at Appomattox Court House.

COLORS OF THE 60th REGIMENT, N. Y. S. V.

Two Flags.

---

1. *Regimental Banner*, blue silk; painted arms State of New York, with Washington's Head-Quarters (Newburgh), and other Hudson River views in back ground; inscribed, "60th Regt. N. Y. S. V." The words "Jehovah Nisi" (the Lord our Banner) embroidered; original staff, spear-head gone.

2. *National Flag*, silk; faded; worn.

Flag No. 2, was borne at Chancellorsville, in which battle the Regiment lost eleven killed and fifty wounded and missing; at Gettysburg, where the Regiment lost thirteen killed and thirty-seven wounded, and had the honor of capturing two rebel battle-flags (one belonging to JONES' Brigade) and fifty-six prisoners; and in the battles of Chattanooga, viz.: Lookout Mountain, where the Regiment lost five killed and thirty-two wounded (among the latter Major W. M. THOMAS, severely), and captured Gen. WALTHAL'S sword, his Brigade battle-flag, two pieces of artillery, and two hundred prisoners; Missionary Ridge, Peavine Creek, and Ringgold. At the latter place the Regiment lost four killed and thirteen wounded. At the battle of Lookout Mountain, Sergeant LEAHY, who bore it, being twice hit, fell to the ground. Sergeant BUCK sprang forward and seized it, and with a coolness and bravery undisturbed by the whiz of bullets, steadily bore it in advance of the Regiment, and planted it at last on that part of the mountain where the enemy had boasted that the Stars and Stripes should never wave again. He has since been promoted to the rank of Captain.

The 60th Regiment was raised in St. Lawrence, Franklin and Clinton counties, and is known as the "St. Lawrence County Regiment." It left Ogdensburgh Nov. 1st, and the State Nov. 4th, 1861, and was on duty at Baltimore, Harper's Ferry, Shenandoah Valley, and other points until September, 1862, when it participated in the battle of Antietam, and suffered severe loss in the death of Col. WM. B. GOODRICH. It remained in the Army of the Potomac until the 25th September, 1863, when it was transferred, with the Twelfth Army Corps, to the Department of the Cumberland, and participated in the battles above mentioned. It reënlisted as a veteran command, Dec. 24, 1863, and under Gen. SHERMAN participated in the battles of Resaca, Mt. Hope Church (where it lost eight killed and fifty-two wounded), and Peach Tree Creek, and was the first Regiment to plant its banner over the Court House in Atlanta, contesting for that honor in a race with the 111th Pa. Vols. At Chancellorsville, it was commanded by Lt.-Col. J. A. C. O. REDINGTON; in all the subsequent battles mentioned, by Col. ABEL GODARD. During the march from Atlanta to Savannah, it was commanded by Major THOMAS ELLIOTT, which latter place it was one of the first to enter, belonging as it did to the 3d Brigade, of the 2d Division of the Twentieth Army Corps. It is at the present time commanded by Lieut.-Col. LESTER S. WILLSON, who has been promoted from the ranks for soldierly conduct and gallantry.

Represented by Lieut.-Col. LESTER S. WILLSON.

COLORS OF THE 61st REGIMENT, N. Y. S. V.

Five Flags.

---

1. *National Flag*, silk; with piece of original broken staff.

This Flag was presented to the Regiment by the City of New York, in 1861. It was in the battles of Yorktown, Fair Oaks, Peach Orchard, Savage's Station, White Oak Swamp, Charles City Cross Roads, Malvern Hill, Antietam, Charlestown, Snicker's Gap and Fredericksburgh. At the battle of Fair Oaks, the Color-Bearer and four of the Color-Guard were killed. At Antietam, the Color-Bearer, FRANK ALDRICH, was killed, and flag-staff shot in three pieces.

2. *National Flag*, silk; with original staff.

This Flag was presented to the Regiment by the City of New York, in 1861. It was used as the parade Flag until the Peninsula campaign, when it was laid aside. In the spring of 1863, it was brought into service, and was carried through the battles of Chancellorsville, Gettysburg, Auburn, Bristow Station and Mine Run. At Gettysburg, the Color-Bearer and two of the Color-Guard were wounded.

3. *National Flag*, silk; field all gone and three-fourths of stripes.

This Flag was carried by the Regiment during the campaign of 1864, and waved triumphantly over the bloody fields of

Wilderness, Todd's Tavern, Po River, Cobbany Bridge, Tolopotamy Creek, Coal Harbor, Petersburgh (three), Deep Bottom (two), White's Tavern, Spottsylvania, South Anna, Reams' Station.

4. *National Flag*, silk; original staff. Inscribed on plate, "61st Regt. N. Y. S. V., 1863. Presented by the City of New York."

5. *Regimental Banner*, blue silk, emblazoned with arms and motto of the United States, and "61st N. Y. Vol. Regiment, Infantry." Presented by the City of New York.

These Flags were in every action in which the Second Corps took part from Oct., 1864. They were first unfurled on the ramparts of Fort McGilvery, in front of Petersburgh, and from thence in the following engagements: Hatcher's Run, Petersburgh to March 25th, Boydtown Road (two), Sutherland's Plantation, Sailor's Creek, Cumberland Church and the surrender of LEE. During this campaign, four of the Color-Guard were disabled (two killed).

The 61st Regiment was organized in the city of New York, Oct. 8th, 1861, by consolidation of the "1st Regiment, Clinton Guard," and the "Astor Regiment." One company was from Albany, and one from Hamilton, and portions of several companies were from different parts of the State. The majority of the Regiment, however, was recruited in New York. It took part in the following actions: Fair Oaks, Peach Orchard and Savage's Station, White Oak Swamp, Charles City Cross Roads, Malvern Hill, Antietam, Fredericksburgh, Chancellorsville, Gettysburg, Auburn, Bristow Station, Mine Run, Wilderness, Todd's Tavern, Po River, Cobbany Bridge, Tolopotamy Creek, Coal Harbor, Petersburgh (three), Deep Bottom (two), White's Tavern, Spottsylvania, South Anna,

Reams' Station, and the closing battles of the war in the vicinity of Richmond. At Antietam it captured the Flag of a Georgia Regiment, inscribed "Williamsburgh," "Seven Pines," and also about three hundred prisoners. It has given to the nation devoted service, and to history a noble record of its honored dead.

COLORS OF THE 63d REGIMENT, N. Y. S. V.

Three Flags.

---

1. *National Flag*, silk; almost entirely destroyed; original staff; inscribed on plate, "63d Regiment, N. Y. S. V., 1863. Presented by the City of New York."

2, 3. *Guidons*, blue silk; "63d" in center.

The 63d Regiment was organized in the city of New York in the fall of 1861, from recruits raised in that city and in Boston and Albany. It was first called the "Independent Irish Regiment," and subsequently the "Third Irish Regiment." It arrived in the field on the 1st of December, 1861, and was assigned to the Irish Brigade under command of General MEAGHER. In the spring of 1862, it was made a part of the 2d Brigade, 1st Division, Second Army Corps, and continued in that position during the whole history of the Army of the Potomac. It has served under MCCLELLAN, POPE, BURNSIDE, HOOKER, MEADE and GRANT; has never lost a Color; and, by general orders No. 10 (March 7, 1865), is entitled to write upon its Banners the names of twenty-three battles, in addition to those in which it has taken part since that time. In consequence of losses in the service, the balance of all the original companies were consolidated into "A" and "B," June 10th, 1863; and four new companies were added in 1863–4.

Represented by Col. R. C. BENTLEY and Capt. M. O'SULLIVAN.

COLORS OF THE 64th REGIMENT, N. Y. S. V.

Three Flags.

---

1. *National Flag*, bunting; worn; staff gone.
2. *National Flag*, silk; much worn and field and stripes disfigured and destroyed; name of Regiment, &c., inscribed; staff gone.
3. *Regimental Banner*, blue silk; two-thirds gone; arms of State of New York originally painted in center, over which were the words "64th Reg. N. Y. Vols.;" under arms the words, "Presented by the Board of Supervisors of Cattaraugus county."

The Flags here presented have been almost destroyed in the service. The *first* was in the siege of Yorktown, and the battles of Fair Oaks, Gaines' Mills, Savage's Station, Peach Orchard, White Oak Swamp, Glendale, Malvern Hill, Antietam, Fredericksburgh, Chancellorsville and Gettysburg. The *second* and *third* were presented to the Regiment by the Board of Supervisors of Cattaraugus county, and were in actions at Gettysburg, Williamsport, Snicker's Gap, Manassas Gap, Auburn Hill, Bristow Station, Mine Run, Wilderness, Po River, Spottsylvania, North Anna, Tolopotamy, South Anna, Guinney's Station, Coal Harbor, Petersburgh (four), Strawberry Plains, Deep Bottom (two), Reams' Station and Hatcher's Run. In each of these engagements the Regiment lost men in killed or wounded.

At Gettysburg, the National Color, No. 1, was carried by

CHAUNCEY MCKOON of Company B, who was severely wounded in the thigh. It was then taken by EDMUND STONE of Company D, who was killed. It was then raised by Sergeant BLACKMORE, who carried it through the remainder of the battle. THOMAS J. ZIBBLE, Corporal of Company F, and ALBERT EMPSEY, Corporal of Company E, were wounded in the same battle while carrying the National Color No. 2.

The organization of the 64th or "First Cattaraugus Regiment," was formally commenced on the 16th of August, 1861. It was composed of seven companies from Cattaraugus county, and one each from the counties of Allegany, Tompkins and Tioga. It left Elmira for Washington, Dec. 10th, 1861; remained in camp in the vicinity of Washington until Jan. 7th, 1862, when it entered upon the campaign of that year. The engagements in which it has participated have been stated. In the battle at Chancellorsville, while imperfectly intrenched, the Regiment repulsed three successive charges by a Brigade of Georgia troops, and captured a number of prisoners who were astonished to find that they had been repulsed and captured by a single Regiment of New York men. In front of the intrenchments, after the battle, 120 men of the 16th Georgia were found dead and were buried there, besides several of other Regiments. The 64th lost 33 men in killed and wounded. Up to August, 1863, it lost 428 in killed and wounded. At Spottsylvania (May 12), the Colors of the 44th Virginia were captured by Sergeant MARSH, of Company B.

Number of commissions issued by the Governor to this Regiment: Colonels, 4; Lieutenant-Colonels, 5; Majors, 7; Adjutants, 4; Quartermasters, 7; Surgeons, 3; Assistant-Surgeons, 4; Chaplain, 1; Captains, 42; First Lieutenants, 54; Second Lieutenants, 66. Total, 197.

COLORS OF THE 71st REGIMENT, N. Y. S. V.

One Flag.

---

1. *National Flag*, silk; inscribed "Jackson Reg't, N. Y. V.;" with original staff.

This Flag was borne in the battles of Stafford Court House, Fair Oaks (June 1st, 12th and 25th), Charles City Cross Roads (June 29th, 30th), Malvern Hill (July 1st and August 4th), Bristow Station, 2d Bull Run, Chantilly and Fredericksburgh.

The 71st Regiment, or "Jackson Light Infantry," was the second Regiment of the "Excelsior (SICKLES') Brigade." It was organized in New York in the summer of 1861, and was composed of volunteers recruited in New York, Newark and Orange, N. J., Philadelphia, Pa., Olean, N. Y., Colchester, Mass., Kingston, N. Y., and in other places. In bayonet charges, in hand to hand conflicts, in valor on the field and in privations and sufferings in trenches and in marches, this Regiment — as well as the noble Brigade of which it was a part — has a history of the highest honor.

COLORS OF THE 75th REGIMENT, N. Y. S. V.

Two Flags.

---

1. *National Flag*, silk; three-quarters gone; original staff, broken by bullets; original cord and tassels.
2. *Regimental Banner*, blue silk; embroidered with coat of arms of the State of New York, and "75th Regiment, N. Y. S. V.;" original staff, cord and tassels. Flag and staff shattered and marked by bullets. Presented to the Regiment by the ladies of Auburn.

"Returned from the field, shivered, torn and riddled, but with honor," is the brief but eloquent record of these Flags. They have never fallen in the face of the enemy. At Port Hudson, the gallant Color-Bearer, who received the National Flag from the ladies of Auburn, was killed, a bullet from the enemy piercing his heart. As he fell, the Colors were snatched from his death grasp by a Corporal, who waved them in defiance.

The 75th Regiment was organized at Auburn, N. Y., Nov. 14th, 1861, from volunteers recruited principally in Cayuga and Onondaga counties, and was known as the "Second Auburn Regiment." It constituted a part of the expedition sent to Pensacola and occupied Santa Rosa Island during the bombardment of Fort Pickens. It was transferred to the Department of the Gulf, then under command of General BUTLER, and served in several important expeditions. It formed part of General WEITZEL's Brigade on the Red

River and before Port Hudson, and was the first Regiment to enter the latter place after its surrender to General BANKS. On the Sabine Pass expedition, two companies (B and G), acting as sharp-shooters, were captured on board the gunboat Clifton, when she grounded in front of the rebel batteries. On its return to New Orleans it was converted into mounted infantry and took part in the second expedition through Northern Louisiana. It reënlisted, Jan. 1st, 1864, as veteran Cavalry, to serve in the Department of the Gulf.

COLORS OF THE 76th REGIMENT, N. Y. S. V.

One Flag.

---

1. *National Flag*, silk; in tatters; original staff gone.

This Flag was presented to the Regiment, on the steps of the Capitol in Albany, on its departure for the field, by Mrs. CAMPBELL, of York Mills, Oneida Co., with public ceremonies. It was carried until December, 1863, during which time it was borne in the battles of Rappahannock Station, Warrenton, Sulphur Springs, Gainesville, 2d Bull Run, South Mountain, Antietam, Upperville, Fredericksburgh, Chancellorsville, Gettysburg and Mine Run. It received fifteen musket balls and one twelve-pound shot through it in action. The Color-Bearer, Sergeant CHAMP, was killed at South Mountain. At Gettysburg, the Color-Bearer was wounded just as the Regiment was falling back, and came near being captured, but was rescued by Private JOHN STEPHENS, of Company H, who left the ranks under the fire of the enemy, and recovered the Flag in safety.

In the campaign of 1864-5, it was in all the battles of the Fifth Corps. About 100 men reënlisted in Jan., 1864, and the Regiment was made up by transfers and conscripts, having had over 2,000 names on its rolls. In Jan., 1865, its veterans were consolidated with the 147th, and subsequently with the 91st, and came home with the latter Regiment.

The organization of the 76th, or "Cortland Regiment," was

commenced at Cortland village, N. Y., and embraced volunteers from the counties of Cortland, Tompkins, Tioga and Madison. Its head-quarters were removed to Albany, Dec. 18th, 1861, where two of its companies were transferred to other organizations, and the balance consolidated with volunteers for the 39th Otsego or Cherry Valley Regiment, raised in the counties of Otsego, Chenango and Schoharie. It left Albany, Jan. 17th, 1862, but did not enter into active service in the field until August 9th, when it joined the forces under General POPE at Culpepper Court House. The battles in which the Regiment was engaged, up to the close of the campaign of 1863, have already been stated.

Represented by Capt. ED. B. COCHRANE.

COLORS OF THE 77th REGIMENT, N. Y. S. V.

Six Flags.

---

1. *Regimental Banner*, blue silk; original staff. The design, painted upon each side (now torn and defaced) was the number of the Regiment, and arms of the State and motto, at the side of which was represented the surrender of Burgoyne in 1777, upon which occasion the American Stars and Stripes are said to have been first displayed. Presented to the Regiment by the sons of Saratoga county, resident in New York, upon its departure for the field, Nov. 29th, 1861.

This Flag was carried in the battle of Lee's Mills, the siege of Yorktown, battles of Mechanicsville, Golden's Farm, Garnet's Hill, White Oak Swamp, Crampton Pass, Antietam, Fredericksburgh, Marye's Heights and Gettysburg. The bearers were Sergeant ISAAC BEMIS, and afterwards Corporal MICHAEL MCWILLIAMS. In the charge up Marye's Heights, one of the Color-Guard was killed, and the Flag torn into shreds by a shell.

2. *Guidon;* staff gone. Two Guidons were presented with the Regimental Banner and were used during the same period. That on the right side of the line was crimson, and that on the left blue. The crimson Guidon is returned.

3. *National Flag*, silk; about half gone; end ragged; the field in ribbons and but little left; bears the inscriptions, "Winchester, Sept. 19, 1864; Fisher's Hill, Sept. 22, 1864; Cedar Creek, Oct. 19, 1864." Original staff, the top of which was shot off in the Wilderness, May 6, 1864.

This Flag was presented to the Regiment by the ladies of Temple Grove Seminary, Saratoga Springs, Nov. 29, 1861, and was carried during three years' service. The lettering was placed upon it after the Regiment left the field, in accordance with an order from General SHERIDAN to the Army of the Shenandoah. In the battle of Chancellorsville the field was torn out by a shell from the enemy's cannon. Among its bearers in battle Corporal JOSEPH MURRER was instantly killed at Antietam; Corporal MICHAEL MCWILLIAMS was killed in the Wilderness (May 6); Corporal HORRIGAN, of the Color-Guard, was killed at Cedar Creek (Oct. 19); and Corporal HENRY MYRES was shot through the right hand in the Wilderness (May 10). It was in every battle in which the Sixth Corps took part, up to Nov., 1864, including Fort Stevens (Washington, D. C.), Winchester, Fisher's Hill and Cedar Creek.

4. *National Flag*, silk; "77th Reg't N. Y. S. V.," embroidered.

5, 6. *Guidons*, blue silk; faded; Corps badge of Sixth Corps in center in white, on which is "77."

These Colors were in service in the Battalion which the 77th left in the field, from Nov., 1864, to the return of the Battalion in July, 1865. They were in the charge at Petersburgh (April 2), and were the first Colors on the enemy's works.

The 77th Regiment was organized in Saratoga county, and, while forming, was known as the "Bemis Heights Regiment." It had upon its rolls 1,463 men, of whom 73 were killed in action, 40 died of wounds, and 148 died of disease. It was under fire for fifty-six hours at Lee's Mills; was in reserve at Williamsburgh, but advanced in double quick to complete the victory; was in battle at Mechanicsville, where it captured a Guidon belonging to a Georgia Regiment; was at Gaines' Mills, Savage's Station, and the movements before Richmond in 1862, terminating with Malvern Hill. Returning from the Peninsula, it was at 2d Bull Run, Crampton Pass, and Antietam, and closed the service of that year at Fredericksburgh (Dec. 13). In 1863, it was in the mud campaign of Jan. 21; at Marye's Heights (May 3), where it captured the Flag of the 18th Mississippi; at Fredericksburgh, May 4; Gettysburg, July 3; Rappahannock Station, Oct. 20; and at Robinson's Tavern in November following. In the campaign of 1864, it was engaged in the Wilderness, and at Spottsylvania, Coal Harbor, Petersburgh, Fort Stevens, Opequan, Fisher's Hill, and Cedar Creek. The Regiment was then mustered out (Nov., 1864), but left a Battalion in the field, which was engaged in the final assault on Petersburgh, April 2, 1865. The Battalion was mustered out in July, 1865. The 77th followed the entire fortunes of the Army of the Potomac, having been with it at its organization and present at its disbandment.

Represented by Col. W. B. FRENCH, on behalf of the Regiment, and by Lieut.-Col. DAVID J. CAW, on behalf of the Battalion. Carried by members of the Regiment.

COLORS OF THE 78th REGIMENT, N. Y. S. V.

One Flag.

---

1. *National Flag*, silk; nearly all gone; flag-staff has been twice broken by bullets; the lower break has been mended; the upper one is still unrepaired. On silver plate on the staff, "78th Regiment, N. Y. V., 1863. Presented by the City of New York."

This Flag was presented to the Regiment in the summer of 1863, at Fairfax Court House, Va. It was carried in several skirmishes in Virginia, and accompanied the Regiment to the west, where it was borne in the battles of Wauhatchie, Lookout Mountain, Resaca, Dallas, Lost Mountain, Pine Knob, Kenesaw, Peach Tree Creek, and siege of Atlanta; was carried through the campaign to Savannah, and was the first to enter that city; was also carried in the late Carolina campaign. One Color-Bearer was severely wounded at Resaca, and one at Lost Mountain.

The organization of the 78th Regiment was commenced in the fall of 1861, by Colonel S. McKENSIE ELLIOTT, of New York, under the synonym of "Cameron Highlanders." It was subsequently consolidated with companies recruited by General G. A. SCROGGS, at Buffalo, and by Colonel DANIEL ULLMAN, for the Eagle Brigade, and took the field, under the officer last named, in the spring of 1862. Its regimental organization was continued until July 12, 1864, when it was consolidated with the 102d N. Y. Veteran Volunteers. In addition to the engagements and services stated in connection with the Flag here presented, the Regiment was in action at Harper's Ferry, May, 1862, and at Cedar Mountain, Sulphur Springs, Centreville, South Mountain, Antietam, Winchester, Chancellorsville, and Gettysburg. On every field in which it has been engaged, the services of the Regiment have been highly honorable.

COLORS OF THE 80th REGIMENT, N. Y. S. V. (20th N. Y. S. M.)

Two Flags.

---

1. *National Flag*, silk; "20th Regiment, N. Y. S. M., in gilt; original staff gone. Presented to the Regiment by the ladies of Poughkeepsie.

This Flag was in the battles of Norman's Ford, Warrenton Springs, Gainesville, Bull Run 2d (where Colonel PRATT was mortally wounded), Chantilly, South Mountain, Antietam and Fredericksburgh. The Regiment lost 35 killed and 232 wounded, in the campaign of 1862, while fighting under these colors. Its Color-Bearers were repeatedly shot down, and some of its officers were shot while holding the colors.

2. *Regimental Banner*, blue silk; embroidered with eagle, and arms of the State of New York; "20th Regiment, N. Y. S. M., Ulster Guard," in scroll above arms; "Excelsior," in scroll below. Also the words, "Washington, April, 1861, Warrenton, Manassas, Norman's Ford, Chantilly, South Mountain, Antietam." Below all, the words "Presented by the Ladies of Saugerties, N. Y." "Fredericksburgh," affixed on paper in gilt letters. Marked by bullets; staff gone.

While carrying the Flag here presented, Color-Sergeant EDWARD BECKET was shot through the hand, the ball shattering the flag-staff. The gilt eagle was shot from the top of the staff on the third day of the engagement at Gettysburg. It was borne in the battles named in connection with the National Flag of the Regiment, and also at Chancellors ville and at Gettysburg. In the latter battle the Regiment lost 145 officers and men in killed and wounded, and at one time was under the fire of seventy-five to one hundred of the enemy's artillery.

The 80th Regiment, known as the "Ulster Guard," went out originally as the 20th Militia, under the command of the late lamented Colonel GEORGE W. PRATT. The 20th Militia was one of the oldest militia organizations in the State. In February, 1861, it tendered its services to the general government, in case of an outbreak, and was ordered to the field in April of that year, for three months' service. At the expiration of that term it reörganized for three years or the war, and left for the field in the latter part of October. After the battle of Gettysburg, it was assigned to duty with the Provost-Marshal-General of the Army of the Potomac, and, having reënlisted, remained in that department. It has never (except officially) recognized the title of "80th Regiment," regarding its old designation of "20th Militia" an honor to itself and to the State which it has so nobly represented in all the reverses and in all the triumphs of the war.

COLORS OF THE 81st REGIMENT, N. Y. S. V.

Two Flags.

---

1. *National Flag*, bunting.

This Flag was used as the storm Flag of the Regiment. It was flying from the Colonel's tent at Seven Pines when the Regiment fell back with Casey's Division to the second line, May 31, 1862. It was left behind, but being remembered, was returned for and recovered. The Colonel's tent took fire at Northwest Landing, Va., March, 1864, and burned the Flag somewhat.

2. *National Flag*, silk; accompanied by the original staff, which was broken in four places by shot and shell.

This Flag was presented to the Regiment, December 3, 1863, by Mrs. E. C. INGERSOLL, of Lee, Oneida county, N. Y., and was in service from January 1, 1864, to January 1, 1865, in the following engagements, viz.: Violet Station, Drury's Bluff, Coal Harbor, Petersburgh, Fort Harrison and Fair Oaks 2d, and in several skirmishes. The staff was broken in four parts by shot and shell, one of which (a minie ball) struck between the hands of the Color-Sergeant, EVAN MICHAELS, and passed through his body, inflicting a mortal wound. The eagle, surmounting the staff, was carried away by a shot, and not recovered. The Flag shows thirty-six bullet holes, and in its field are two holes made by cannon shot. In carrying this Flag four of the Color-Guard were killed, and fifteen wounded. It is replaced in the regiment by a Flag awarded by the Major-General commanding the Department, for gallant services in the battle at Fort Harrison, where the Regiment captured a redoubt with a battery of artillery, a large number of prisoners and two battle-flags.

The 81st was known as the "Second Oswego Regiment," and was principally from Oswego and Oneida counties. It left the State March 5, 1862, and was in active service until the close of the war. It lost in the last campaign alone, four hundred and eighteen men.

Represented by Colonel JACOB J. DE FOREST.

COLORS OF THE 86th REGIMENT, N. Y. S. V.

Six Flags.

---

1. *National Flag*, merino; lower red, white, and part of second red stripe gone, and also ends of stripes; has about twenty bullet holes in it.

This Flag was presented to company B by the ladies of Addison, Steuben county, N. Y., and was regarded as the property of that company until the battle of Chancellorsville, when its Captain, WILLIAM N. ANGLE, was killed, while gallantly leading his company in a charge on the enemy. It was then adopted by the Regiment. It was always used as the battle-flag of the Regiment until the campaign of 1864, and was in the following engagements, viz.: 2d Bull Run, Manassas Gap, Fredericksburgh, Chancellorsville, Beverly Ford, Gettysburg, Wapping Heights, Auburn, Kelly's Ford, Orange Grove and Mine Run. Four Color-Sergeants were killed while carrying it in battle.

2. *Regimental Banner*, blue silk; in tatters; painted with arms and motto of the United States, and number of Regiment; original staff, cord and tassels.

This Flag was obtained from the general government, in March, 1864, and was carried in the following battles and skirmishes, viz.: Wilderness, Spottsylvania, North Anna, Silver Creek, Petersburgh, Deep Bottom, Hatcher's Run, Coal

Harbor and Weldon railroad — in all, twenty-two engagements.

3. *National Flag*, silk; with staff.
4. *Regimental Banner*, blue silk; with eagle and motto of United States; staff, &c.
5. 6. *Guidons*, with staffs.

These Flags were returned to the Adjutant-General.

The 86th Regiment was organized by Colonel B. P. BAILEY, in the summer of 1861. Eight companies were from Steuben county, one from Chemung, and one from Onondaga. It left the State, November 23, 1861, with a full complement of officers and about 950 men. It reënlisted, December, 1863.

COLORS OF THE 87th REGIMENT, N. Y. S. V.

Three Flags.

---

1. *National Flag*, silk, somewhat worn and faded; staff entire; spear-head gone. Inscribed, in needlework, " 87th Reg., N. Y. S. V." Presented by the City of Brooklyn.
2. *Regimental Banner*, blue silk, painted with the arms of city of New York; beneath which, in scroll, the words " Presented by the City of New York;" above arms, in scroll, the words, "87th Regiment, N. Y. S. V.;" staff and tassels entire; spear-head gone.
3. *Regimental Banner*, white silk, large and rich; in center, in blue and gold, the arms of the city of Brooklyn, and underneath, in scroll, the words, " Presented by the City of Brooklyn;" immediately over the arms, in scroll, the words, " Col. STEPHEN A. DODGE;" above the latter, in scroll, the words, " 87th Regt., Brooklyn Rifles, N. Y. S. V ;" staff and spear-head, the latter broken off.

The 87th Regiment was recruited in Brooklyn, in the fall of 1861, under the auspices of the officers of the 13th N. Y. S. M., on the return of that Regiment from three months' service. It was mustered into the service of the United States, November 20, 1861, and left for Washington on the 2d December, following. Participating in the siege of Yorktown, and in the skirmish at Peach Orchard, it was subsequently in severe action at Williamsburgh and at Fair Oaks, and in several minor engagements. On the withdrawal of the army before Richmond, it joined in the campaign under

General Pope, suffered severely in the 2d battle of Bull Run, and was soon after consolidated with the 40th Regiment, N. Y. V., by order of the War Department. A brief but honorable career.

COLORS OF THE 90th REGIMENT, N. Y. S. V.

One Flag.

---

1. *National Flag*, silk; original staff, cord and tassels. Inscription on plate, "90th Regiment, N. Y. S. V., 1863. Presented by the City of New York."

This Flag was carried by the Regiment from September, 1864, to March, 1865. It bears the marks of many bullets and one piece of shell, and the staff is shattered by some flying missile. The Flag is marked with blood from the death wound of Sergeant JOHN FOLEY, of Company C, Color-Bearer, who was killed at the battle of Cedar Creek, Va.

The 90th Regiment was recruited in New York and Brooklyn, and was organized by the consolidation of the "MCCLELLAN Chasseurs," and the "MCCLELLAN Rifles." It left New York in December, 1861, reënlisted in the summer of 1864, and subsequently served as the 90th Battalion. The Regiment (or parts of it) has participated in the following battles, viz.: Siege of Port Hudson, La., Pleasant Valley, La., Pleasant Hill, La., Cane River, La., Avoyelles Prairie, La., Cox's Plantation, La., Opequan, Va., Fisher's Hill, Va., Cedar Creek, Va.

COLORS OF THE 91st REGIMENT, N. Y. S. V.

One Flag.

---

1. *National Flag*, silk; faded, torn. Inscribed, "Irish Bend, April 14th, 1863; Vermillion Bayou, April 17th, 1863; Port Hudson, May 25th, 27th, and June 14th, 1863; Cox's Plantation, July 13th, 1863." Original staff, broken and brass ornament gone.

This Flag was presented to the 91st Regiment, by Mrs. Col. J. W. HARCOURT, of Albany, on its departure for the seat of war, December, 1861. At Port Hudson (May 27), it was torn in two and the top of the staff carried away, while being borne by Corporal JAMES E. JONES, of Company D, who was wounded in the face by a splinter. Corporal PATRICK H. GARRITY, of Company H, picked up the piece and the spear, and, being wounded in the foot, they were taken by him to the hospital. Subsequently they were returned to Mrs. H., by Colonel VAN ZANDT. The remainder of the Flag and staff were carried by the Regiment until its reënlistment, in 1864, when they were also returned to Mrs. H. In the battle of Irish Bend, the Flag was borne by Sergeant GILL, of Company C, and it was also borne by him at Port Hudson until he was wounded. It was then taken by Corporal JONES; and when he was wounded, by Private TOWNSEND, of Company K. Private TOWNSEND joined the Regiment at Pensacola, having deserted the rebel service (into which he had been pressed) at Mobile. He carried the Flag until the 14th of June, when, in the last battle at Port Hudson, he fell pierced with seven balls, one of which, as was ascertained after the surrender of the rebel forces, was from a gun in the hands of his brother, who was a member of the 10th Alabama, and who recognized him at the instant of discharging his piece. TOWNSEND subsequently died of his wounds. Corporal GARRITY took the Flag from TOWNSEND, and carried it until it was returned to its donor, in 1864.

The 91st Regiment was organized in Albany, of volunteers enlisted, in part, for the "Fredendall Regiment," and for the "Columbia Regiment;" the former under orders issued to Captain J. FREDENDALL, of Albany, and the latter under orders issued to DAVID S. COWLES, of Hudson, N. Y. It left Albany, December 20, 1861; was on duty for some time at Pensacola, and subsequently, under Gen. BANKS, in Louisiana. After its reënlistment it was in the campaign against Richmond, and was in battles on the South Side Railroad (March 28, 29, 30, 31, April 1, 2, 3, 4, 1865), and at Five Forks (May 2). Its last engagement was a skirmish under the tree under which General LEE's command was subsequently surrendered to Lieut.-General GRANT.

COLORS OF THE 92d REGIMENT, N. Y. S. V.

One Flag.

1. *National Flag*, silk; embroidered with name of Regiment and the words "Excelsior Rifle Battalion." Returned by the Regiment, May 11, 1864.

This Flag was used by the Regiment until it was so torn by bullets that it could not be unfurled.

The 92d Regiment was organized in St. Lawrence county. It left the State, February 17, 1862, and that portion of it which remained to be mustered out, returned January 10, 1865. It was engaged in sixteen battles, and in several skirmishes and reconnoisances, and repeatedly received the special commendations of its commanding Generals for the gallantry of its men.

COLORS OF THE 93d REGIMENT, N. Y. S. V.

One Flag.

---

1. *National Flag*, silk; original staff.

This Flag is returned by the 93d Battalion, and is presented by Lieutenant BERTHOLD EMISCH, Acting Adjutant.

The 93d Regiment, or "Morgan Rifles," was composed of companies recruited in the counties of Warren, Washington, Essex, Albany and Columbia. It was organized at Albany, January, 1862, and left for the seat of war under the command of Colonel JOHN S. CROCKER, mustering 38 officers and 983 men. At various times it received recruits to the number of 684, making the aggregate of men upon its rolls, 1,705. On the 29th of June, 1865, near Bailey's Cross Roads, Va., it was mustered out, its rolls embracing the names of 23 officers and 515 men, of whom only 2 officers and 85 men went out with it originally. On the 18th March, 1862, the Regiment was attached to CASEY's Division, PALMER's Brigade, with which it remained during the siege of Yorktown and the battle of Williamsburgh. On the 19th May it was detached and sent to White House Landing, on the Pamunkey river, for provost and guard duty; and on the 21st of May, four companies were detached as Head-Quarters Guard. The Regiment remained at White House Landing until the evacuation of that place, when it rejoined the army at Harrison's Landing—the Head-Quarters Guard meanwhile performing very severe duty during the movements on the Peninsula. The command was united at Meridian Hill, Sept. 3d, and commenced the Maryland campaign, still serving as guard, in which capacity it was present at South Mountain, Antietam, Fredericksburgh, Chancellorsville, Gettysburg, and the movements of the Army of the Potomac, up to January, 1864, when it came home on furlough, having reënlisted. The campaigns of 1864–5 it passed in the field, and was in actions at Wilderness, Spottsylvania, North Anna, Tolopotomy, Coal Harbor, Petersburgh, Strawberry Plains, Deep Bottom, Poplar Spring Church, Boydtown Plank Road, Hatcher's Run, 2d Boydtown Plank Road, Jettersville, Sailor's Creek, High Bridge, and at the surrender of General LEE, at Clover Hill, Va., April 9, 1865. For its gallantry in the Wilderness, and at Spottsylvania, it received the thanks of Generals HANCOCK and BIRNEY in General Orders—praise awarded to no other Regiment in that gallant Corps. In the responsible duties of Head-Quarters Guard, as well as in the field, its record is without blemish.

COLORS OF THE 95th REGIMENT, N. Y. S. V.

One Flag.

---

1. *National Flag*, silk; with silver band on staff, bearing the inscription, "95th Regiment, N. Y. S. V. Presented by the City of New York."

This Flag was sent to the Regiment by the authorities of New York city, August 1, 1863. It was borne through the battles of Mine Run, Wilderness, Spottsylvania, Laurel Hill, North Anna, Tolopotomy Creek, Bottom's Bridge, Bethesda Church, Coal Harbor and Petersburgh, when it became too dilapidated for further use. In the various fights in which it was borne, six Color-Bearers were shot.

The 95th Regiment was organized in the city of New York, under the synonym of "Warren Rifles." It was in action at 2d Bull Run, at South Mountain, at Antietam, at Fredericksburgh, at Gettysburg, in the Wilderness, at Coal Harbor, and in several other actions and skirmishes. The brave and lamented Colonel EDWARD PYE, of Rockland county, died of wounds received while leading this Regiment at Coal Harbor.

COLORS OF THE 96th REGIMENT, N. Y. S. V.

One Flag.

---

1. *National Flag*, bunting.

The Flag here presented was in service until the 23d of November, 1862. In presenting new colors to the Regiment at that time, Colonel GRAY remarked, "That *old Flag* has passed through every conflict in which this Regiment has participated; at Fair Oaks, Chickahominy Swamp, White Oak Swamp, Railroad Bridge, Bottom's Bridge, Long's Bridge, Jones' Ford, Charles City Cross Roads, Harrison's Point. It has fired the hearts of the weary and worn soldiers who have marched and fought beneath it; and as not a single star is injured, so may it be with the States they represent." In the next battle in which the Regiment was engaged, Colonel GRAY was killed, and this Flag accompanied his remains to his former home.

The 96th Regiment was organized at Plattsburgh, N. Y., and was composed of companies raised in Clinton, Essex, Franklin, Warren and Washington counties. It left for the seat of war, March 11, 1862; served on the Peninsula in the siege of Yorktown, and in the battles of Williamsburgh and Fair Oaks, in CASEY's Division; in the battles of Chickahominy Swamp, White Oak Swamp, Railroad Bridge, Bottom's Bridge, Long's Bridge, Jones' Ford, Charles City Cross Roads and Harrison's Point, in PECK's Division; was sent to

Suffolk, Va., in September, 1862, and from thence to Newbern, N. C., and was engaged in that Department in the battles of Kinston, Whitehall and Goldsboro. It reënlisted in the spring of 1864, and on taking the field was assigned to the Eighteenth Corps, Army of the James; subsequently to the Twenty-fourth Corps. The services of the Regiment on the Peninsula were accompanied by great peril and hardships, and won from General PECK a fitting acknowledgment in his General Orders. Colonel CHARLES O. GRAY, one of the most brave and accomplished officers in the service, was killed in the action at Kinston, N. C. (December 14, 1862), while in the act of planting the colors of the Regiment on the enemy's position, on the bridge over the Neuse river.

COLORS OF THE 97th REGIMENT, N. Y. S. V.

(One Flag.)

---

1. *National Flag*, silk; inscribed "Col. WHEELOCK, 97th Conklin Rifles, N. Y." Accompanied by original staff.

This Flag was presented to the Regiment by the ladies of Boonville, March, 1862, and was carried in the battles of Cedar Mountain, Rappahannock Station, Thoroughfare Gap, 2d Bull Run, Chantilly, South Mountain, Antietam, Fredericksburgh, Chancellorsville, Gettysburg and Mine Run.

The 97th Regiment was organized at Boonville, from enlistments in Oneida, Lewis, and Herkimer counties, and was the first of the three years Regiments from Oneida county. It left for Washington in April, 1862, under the command of Colonel (afterwards Brevet Brig.-Gen.) CHARLES WHEELOCK, now deceased. It has been engaged in the following battles and skirmishes, in addition to those already stated, viz.: Wilderness, Spottsylvania, and through to Petersburgh and the final triumph over the rebellion.

COLORS OF THE 98th REGIMENT, N. Y. S. V.

(Three Flags.)

---

1. *National Flag*, silk; worn. Bears the name of the Regiment in gilt letters.

This Flag was presented to the Regiment at Albany, in 1861, on its departure for the seat of war, and was carried by the Regiment during the first two years of its service.

2, 3. *Guidons*, silk.

These Flags were returned to the Adjutant-General.

The 98th Regiment was raised in the counties of Franklin and Wayne. It served in the Peninsular campaign, and formed the advanced guard of the Fourth Corps in the preliminary occupation of Seven Pines, suffered severely in the battle of Fair Oaks, and was engaged in the Seven Days' fight. In December, 1863, it accompanied the expedition under General FOSTER to South Carolina. Here it was consolidated into five companies. It reënlisted in the winter of 1863-4, and came home with General LEDLIE's Brigade, received several new companies and recruits, and again took the field in the campaign against Richmond as a part of the Army of the James. It was in action near Fort Darling (May 16), at Coal Harbor (May 1, 2, 3), and in several minor engagements, and was the *second Regiment that entered the city of Richmond* on its capture.

COLORS OF THE 101st REGIMENT, N. Y. S. V.

(One Flag.)

1. *National Flag*, silk; with original staff.

This Flag was presented to the Regiment by the Union Defense Committee of New York city. It was borne in the battles of Seven Pines (May 31st and June 1st), Peach Orchard, Savage's Station, Chickahominy Swamp, White Oak Swamp, Charles City Cross Roads, Malvern Hill, Groveton, 2d Bull Run, Chantilly and Fredericksburgh.

The 101st Regiment was organized by the consolidation of Regiments recruiting in the counties of Onondaga and Delaware, and left the State, March 9th, 1862. In the winter of 1863–4, it was consolidated with the 27th Regiment, N. Y. S. V. In his report after the battle of Fredericksburgh, Brig.-General BERRY said: "I have also to mention the good conduct of the 101st N. Y. Vols., Colonel CHESTER commanding. They nobly performed their duty during the fight; also as pickets on the night of the retreat. This Regiment, though small in numbers, did good service; and its conduct, together with that of all its officers, was unexceptionable."

COLORS OF THE 102d REGIMENT, N. Y. S. V.

(One Flag.)

---

1. *National Flag*, silk; inscribed in gilt, "102d Regiment, N. Y. S. V." "Cedar Mountain, the Rappahannock, White Sulphur Springs, Antietam." Original staff, with plate inscribed, "Presented by the friends of Colonel W. B. HAYWARD, in the employ of Stone, Stark & Co."

This Flag was borne in the engagements that are inscribed upon it.

The 102d Regiment was organized in the city of New York, by the consolidation of the "Van Buren Light Infantry," and the "Von Beck Rifles." It was composed of volunteers enlisted in the counties of New York, Suffolk, Yates and Ulster, and left for the field, March 10th, 1862, under the command of Colonel THOMAS B. VAN BUREN, who, in consequence of continued illness, was compelled to resign. During the greater part of the time that the Regiment was in the field, it was under the command of Colonel J. C. LANE, who originally went out as its Major. Lieut.-Colonel WILLIAM B. HAYWARD was in command a short time at Harper's Ferry. At Cedar Mountain it was under a heavy fire of artillery and musketry for five hours, and lost 141 officers and men in killed and wounded. At Antietam it was under fire for four hours. At Chancellorsville it lost seventy-four men, and captured three officers and forty men, together with the Color-Sergeant and the battle-flag of the 12th Georgia. At Gettysburg, it was one of the New York Regiments that successfully resisted EWELL's Corps, and left more of the enemy's dead outside of the rifle-pits than there were defenders in them. In September, 1863, the Regiment accompanied its Corps (the Twelfth) to Nashville, Tenn., and subsequently took part in the battles of Lookout Mountain, Missionary Ridge, Ringgold, Rocky Faced Ridge, Resaca, Dallas (where it was seven days and nights in the trenches, and expended 20,000 rounds of ammunition), Allatoona Bridge, Ackworth Village, and Pine Hill. In this campaign the Regiment lost over one-fourth of its whole number of fighting men. On the 12th of July, about two miles from Atlanta, it was consolidated with the 78th N. Y. V. (the new organization retaining the old number (102), united in the siege of Atlanta, marched from Atlanta to Savannah, and served in the subsequent movements of the army under the command of General SHERMAN.

COLORS OF THE 103d REGIMENT, N. Y. S. V.

(Two Flags.)

---

1. *Regimental Banner*, silk; one-third gone; shield in center, surmounted by eagle, over which, in scroll, "103d Regiment N. Y. S. V.;" under shield, "Excelsior" in scroll; in upper corner, near the staff, are the words, "Presented by WILLIAM H. SEWARD, March 1, 1862;" the whole embroidered.
2. *National Flag*, silk, worn; union rent in several places, portion of middle gone; inscribed "103d Regt. N. Y. S. V."

These colors were presented to the 103d Regiment by Hon. WM. H. SEWARD. They were carried by the Regiment on the expedition under Gen. BURNSIDE to North Carolina; from thence, on transfer, to the Army of the Potomac, were under Gen. MCCLELLAN at South Mountain, Sharpsburgh and Antietam, and in the terrible charge on Stone Bridge. They were in the engagement under Gen. BURNSIDE at Fredericksburgh; under Gen. HOOKER at Chancellorsville; under Gen. MEADE at Gettysburg; under Gen. GILMORE in the capture of Fort Wagner and Battery Gregg; under Gen. SHERIDAN in Shenandoah Valley; and under Gen. BUTLER at Bermuda Hundred.

The 103d was a German Regiment, and was organized in the city of New York under the synonym of "Seward Infantry." It left the State March 5, 1862, with 1,183 men, under command of Col. F. VON EGLOFFSTEIN; and at muster out in March, 1865, left 285 reënlisted men in the field.

COLORS OF THE 104th REGIMENT, N. Y. S. V.

(One Flag.)

---

1. *Regimental Banner*, blue silk; embroidered with "Wadsworth Guard, N. Y. S. V.," and State arms and motto; on ferrule, "Presented to the 104th Regiment, N. Y. S. V., Wadsworth Guard, by Gen. JAMES S. WADSWORTH, April, 1862." Original staff.

This Flag was carried through the actions of Cedar Mountain, Rappahannock Station, Thoroughfare Gap, 2d Bull Run, South Mountain, Antietam, Fredericksburgh, Chancellorsville and Gettysburg. One of its bearers was severely wounded at South Mountain, and another at Antietam. At Gettysburg, seven of the Sergeants and Color-Guard were killed and wounded, and the Flag barely saved by great vigilance — the National Flag (its companion) having been torn from its staff and stamped in the ground to conceal it from the enemy's notice.

The 104th Regiment was organized at Geneseo, Livingston county, N. Y., by Col. JOHN RORBACH. Seven companies were from Livingston, and three from Rensselaer county. It left for the seat of war, March 22d, 1862. It lost 94 officers and enlisted men at 2d Bull Run; at Antietam, 76; at Fredericksburgh, 53; at Gettysburg, 219; and on the first of January, 1864, had 315 men on its rolls out of an original total of 917.

COLORS OF THE 105th REGIMENT, N. Y. S. V.

(One Flag.)

---

1. *National Flag*, silk; on one side of field, arms of United States painted, inscribed "105th Regt., N. Y. S. V.," and "Justice shall triumph," in embroidery. "Cedar Mountain, Aug. 9th, 1862," "Rappahannock Station, Aug. 23d, 1863," "Thoroughfare Gap, Aug. 28th, 1862," "2d Bull Run, Aug. 30th, 1862," "Chantilly, Sept. 1st, 1862," "South Mountain, Sept. 14th, 1862," "Antietam, Sept. 17th, 1862," "Fredericksburgh, Dec. 13th, 1862," painted.

This Flag was in the principal battles, the names of which are inscribed upon it. Seven Color-Bearers were killed or wounded while carrying it; it is marked by thirty-four bullets and a piece of shell, and its staff was cut in two by a ball. It was presented to the Regiment by the ladies of Le Roy, Genesee county.

The 105th Regiment was recruited in the counties of Madison and Genesee, in the fall and winter of 1861–2. It left the State March 31st, 1862, and was in nine battles before it had been in the field nine months. By active and meritorious service, it became greatly reduced in numbers, and was consolidated with the 94th N. Y. S. V.

COLORS OF THE 107th REGIMENT, N. Y. S. V.

(Two Flags.)

1. *National Flag*, silk; in tatters; original staff broken.
2. *Regimental Banner*, blue silk; in tatters; originally painted with arms and motto of United States, and number of Regiment.

These Flags were returned to the Adjutant-General.

The 107th Regiment was recruited in Chemung, Schuyler and Steuben counties, and was organized at Elmira. It was the first Regiment that left the State under the calls of July and August, 1862, and received from Gov. MORGAN one of a series of prize flags which he awarded. It reached the field a few days previous to the battle of Antietam, in which it took part, as well as in the subsequent battles of the Army of the Potomac, in the campaign of 1863, including Chancellorsville and Gettysburg. It was then assigned to duty in the West as a part of the Twentieth Corps, and was in all the battles and marches of SHERMAN'S army from Chattanooga to Raleigh, N. C. The Flag of this Regiment was the first to wave over the Georgia State House at Milledgeville.

COLORS OF THE 108th REGIMENT, N. Y. S. V.

(Four Flags.)

---

1. *Regimental Banner*, blue silk; very little left; originally painted with arms and motto of United States and number of Regiment; top of staff broken and part of it gone.

This was the first Flag which the Regiment carried. It was received by the Regiment, from General ARTHUR, Quartermaster-General, while on its way to Washington, August 21st, 1862. At the battle of Antietam it was pierced by 69 bullets, and its center was rent in twain by a shell.

2. *National Flag*, silk; almost entirely destroyed; staff broken and held by splints.

3. *Regimental Banner*, blue silk, double; on one side arms of United States and " 108th N. Y. V., Monroe Co., N. Y;" on the other, arms of the State of New York, and " Presented by the Ladies of Brighton, Monroe Co., N. Y." " In God we trust." Staff broken by bullets. Received by the Regiment at Harper's Ferry, October, 1862.

4. *National Flag*, silk; nearly new; with staff.

These Flags were returned to the Adjutant-General. They are entitled to have inscribed upon them the following battles, viz.: Antietam, Fredericksburgh, Chancellorsville, Bristow Station, Mine Run, Gettysburg, Wilderness, Spottsylvania, Tolopotomy, Po River, North Anna, Coal Harbor,

Petersburgh, Deep Bottom, Boydtown Road, Strawberry Plains, Reams' Station.

The 108th Regiment was recruited in Monroe county, between the 10th of July and the 15th of August, 1862, and was the second Regiment organized under the calls of that year. It was assigned to the 3d Division, Second Army Corps, and in its first battle (Antietam) captured one battle-flag and 168 prisoners, including nine commissioned officers, and lost 196 in killed, wounded and missing. At Fredericksburgh it lost 53, and in every engagement in which it subsequently participated, it sustained the reputation which it won in those hard-fought battles.

COLORS OF THE 111th REGIMENT, N. Y. S. V.

(Four Flags.)

1. *National Flag*, silk.
2. *Regimental Banner*, blue silk; emblazoned with arms and motto of United States; original staff.
3. 4. *Guidons*, silk.

These Flags were returned to the Adjutant-General.

The 111th Regiment was recruited in the counties of Wayne and Cayuga, and was mustered in at Auburn, in August, 1862. It was included in the surrender by Colonel Miles, at Harper's Ferry, and was not again in the field until January, 1863. It joined the Second Corps in June, 1863, and fought in the battles of Gettysburg, Auburn, Bristow Station, Robinson's Tavern, Mine Run, Wilderness, and in all the marches and battles of the Second Corps to the disbandment of the Army of the Potomac.

COLORS OF THE 112th REGIMENT, N. Y. S. V.

(One Flag.)

---

1. *Regimental Banner*, blue silk; almost entirely destroyed; staff broken and top gone; originally painted with arms of the State of New York and motto, and number of Regiment.

This Flag was presented to the Regiment at Suffolk, Va., in the name of the ladies of Chautauqua county, and was carried by the Regiment until the fall of 1864, when, having become badly worn, it was returned to its donors.

The 112th Regiment was recruited at Chautauqua as a part of the quota of that county, under the calls of July and August, 1862, and left the State on the 13th September, of that year, with 1,013 officers and enlisted men. It was at Suffolk, Va., during the winter and spring of 1862–3, and participated in many skirmishes and battles in that department. In August, 1863, it was transferred to the Department of the South, and participated in the operations on Morris Island, which resulted in the capture of Forts Wagner and Gregg, and the demolition of Fort Sumter. In February, 1864, it was transferred to Jacksonville, Fla., and in April following, was made a part of the 2d Division of the Tenth Army Corps of the Army of the James. In May, the 2d Division was transferred to the Eighteenth Corps, fought in the battle at Coal Harbor, and subsequently returned to the Tenth Corps. In November, it accompanied General BUTLER to New York city, and in December, formed part of the expedition to capture Fort Fisher. It accompanied the second expedition against Fort Fisher, under General TERRY, and claims the honor, in common with the 3d, the 117th, and 142d N. Y., of being the first to enter the Fort, under Gen. CURTIS. Thence to Wilmington and Raleigh, and the subsequent surrender of General JOHNSTON. It was mustered out June 14, 1865, with an honorable record of services performed in some of the most brilliant operations of the war.

COLORS OF THE 113th REGIMENT, N. Y. S. V.

(One Flag.)

---

1. *Regimental Banner*, silk; with name of Regiment and the United States arms and motto painted on each side.

This Flag was one of the five prize banners presented by Gov. MORGAN to different Regiments in 1862, and was placed in the hands of the Regiment, Aug. 20th, of that year. Immediately after reaching Washington, the Regiment was divided up and sent to garrison eight different fortifications. It was subsequently changed from infantry to artillery, and is now known as the "7th N. Y. Heavy Artillery." The Flag here presented was never used in the field.

The 113th Regiment was recruited in Albany, in the summer of 1862, and went out as the "Albany Regiment." In the campaign against Richmond, just closed, it was ordered to the front as infantry, May 15, 1864, and performed important service in the Wilderness, where it suffered severely, at Coal Harbor, at Reams' Station, and before Petersburgh. Under the banner of this regiment, two noble sons of Albany, Col. LEWIS O. MORRIS, and Major EDWARD A. SPRINGSTEED, exchanged their lives for national immortality.

COLORS OF THE 114th REGIMENT, N. Y. S. V.

Two Flags.

---

1. *National Flag*, silk; a large portion gone; was inscribed with names of battles of which only "Bisland, April," and "Port Hudson, May 24th and 27th," remain; original staff.

2. *Regimental Banner*, blue silk; in good condition; arms of the State of New York and number of Regiment painted; original staff.

These colors are returned by Capt. JAMES F. FITTS, by whom they are presented.

The 114th Regiment was raised in the counties of Chenango and Madison, in August and September, 1862. It left the State September 8th, and remained at Baltimore until November 8th, when it proceeded to Fortress Monroe and joined Gen. BANKS' expedition. It disembarked in Louisiana in January, 1863; participated in BANKS' and FRANKLIN'S Western Louisiana campaigns of that year, and in the reduction of Port Hudson. It was in the battle at Bisland, April 12 and 13, 1863, and in the second assault on Port Hudson, June 14, 1863, where it lost eighty in killed and wounded — among the former, Col. ELISHA B. SMITH. On the Red River expedition it was engaged in the battles of Sabine Cross Roads, Pleasant Hill, Cane River Crossing, and Mansura. It returned to Washington with the Nineteenth Corps (July, 1864) and assisted in the defense of the Capital. It was attached to SHERIDAN'S army during the Shenandoah Valley campaign, and took part in the battles of Opequan, Fisher's Hill, New Market, and Cedar Creek. At Opequan it lost 190 officers and men, out of 350 engaged; and at Cedar Creek it lost 119 officers and men, out of 250 engaged. It took the field with an aggregate of 1,017, and received about 100 recruits. About 360 were mustered out with the Regiment, June 8th, 1865.

COLORS OF THE 115th REGIMENT, N. Y. S. V.

Six Flags.

---

1. *National Flag*, silk; no staff; much worn and tattered; three-fifths gone; lower third of union wanting; lower half and end of stripes gone.

2. *Regimental Banner*, silk; no staff; rent in center; torn from side to side, eagle and shield in center with national motto in scroll beneath, and thirty-four stars in field above. It bears the inscription, "115th N. Y. Vol. Regiment, Infantry," in scroll.

In transmitting these Flags to the archives of the State, Col. SAMMONS writes as follows: "The colors deposited in your department, belonging to the 115th Regiment, New York Volunteers, which I had the honor to command, were carried by the Regiment, and I may say gallantly supported, in the following battles, to wit:

Maryland Heights, Sept. 13, 1862; Olustee, Florida, Feb. 20, 1864; Chester Heights, Va., May 7, 1864; Keer Bottom, May 10, 1864; Proctor's Farm, May 12, 1864; Drury's Bluff, May 16, 1864; Coal Harbor, June 1, 1864; Petersburgh, July 30, 1864; Deep Bottom, Aug. 16, 1864; Chapin's Farm, Sept. 29, 1864; Darbytown Road, Sept. 29, 1864; Fort Fisher, N. C., Jan. 15, 1865; Wilmington, N. C., Feb. 22, 1865.

"The National Flag (No. 1) was presented to the Regiment by the ladies of the 15th Senatorial District, Aug. 20, 1862. The Regimental Banner (No. 2) was presented by the State authorities while the Regiment was organizing at Camp Fonda, Montgomery county.

"The foregoing list of battles, in which the 115th was engaged, number thirteen (13) — the number of the original thirteen States of the Union of 1776. The Regiment has also been engaged in very many "skirmishes," as they are called in the great army of the Potomac, in which the losses were greater than in engagements which other armies have often dignified by the name of battles. The Regiment also manned the works and rifle pits in front of Petersburgh, Va., during forty-five consecutive days and nights in the months of June and July, 1864, under a constant fire of musketry, shot and shell, and suffered a loss in killed and wounded, averaging, at least, three per day during that entire period.

"These banners, tattered, soiled, and blood-stained, bear just evidence of the toil, danger, and privations through which this Regiment has passed."

3. *Regimental Banner*, blue silk; in good condition; arms of United States, and number of Regiment painted; original staff.

4. *National Flag*, silk; new; inscribed with names of battles; original staff.

5. 6. *Guidons*, bunting; with staffs.

These Flags were returned to the Adjutant-General. They are represented by Lieut.-Col. N. J. JOHNSON, and are carried by Sergt. JAMES ENGLISH, who lost an arm while supporting them in the field.

COLORS OF THE 117th REGIMENT, N. Y. S. V.

Five Flags.

---

1. *Regimental Banner,* blue silk; nearly all gone but fringe; original staff broken.
2. *National Flag,* silk; all gone but fringe; original staff;
3. *Regimental Banner,* blue silk; new; emblazoned with arms and motto of United States; original staff.
4. 5. *Guidons,* silk.

These Flags were returned to the Adjutant-General without history.

The 117th Regiment was recruited in Oneida county, in July and August, 1862. It returned from the field, June, 1865, with 350 men.

COLORS OF THE 118th REGIMENT, N. Y. S. V.

Three Flags.

---

1. *National Flag*, silk; only a fragment left; original staff; spear-head gone.
2. *Regimental Banner*, blue silk; only a fragment remaining; original staff.
3. *National Flag*, silk; inscribed in gilt, "118th Regt. N. Y. Vols., and "Suffolk," "South Anna," "Coal Harbor," "Fort Harrison," "Bermuda," "Swift Creek," "Petersburgh," "Fair Oaks," "Drury's Bluff," "Crater," "Richmond."

The National (1) and the Regimental were with the Regiment during its entire term of service. The new National was received under orders issued by Gen. BUTLER, with its inscriptions. They were returned by the Regiment, after its muster out of service, June 13, 1865.

The 118th, or "Adirondack Regiment," was organized at Plattsburgh, and mustered into service, Aug. 27th, 1862. It was composed of three companies from Warren, four from Clinton, and three from Essex county, and had an aggregate of 986 men. It received about 350 recruits, and returned home with only 323, including officers and men. It was on duty at Suffolk, Va., at Gloucester Point, Norfolk and Portsmouth until April, 1864, when it joined the Army of the James, and remained in that command until the close of the war. At Drury's Bluff, Chapin's Farm and Fair Oaks, it lost one-half of the men with which it entered each fight. It was selected by Gen. DEVENS, to be armed with "Spencer's Repeating Rifle," and subsequently formed the skirmishers covering the advance of the 3d Division, Twenty-fourth Corps, was acting as such when Richmond was finally occupied, and was *the first organized Federal Infantry in that city.* It was on the Deep Bottom raid, in HECKMAN'S Brigade, and marched 38 miles in one day in heavy marching order. In a letter to Gov. FENTON on the muster out of the Regiment, Gen. DEVENS writes:

"The 118th N. Y. Volunteers came into the service of the United States in August, 1862. After a few months of Provost duty in the city of Washington, it was transferred to the department of Virginia, and has always remained with the troops of this department. It bore its part in the siege of Suffolk, and in the expedition of Gen. DIX up the Peninsula, and subsequently in the command of Gen. GETTY at Newport News, in the year 1863. Its principal and most severe campaigns have been since the spring of 1864, when it was assigned to the Eighteenth Corps, then commanded by Gen. WM. F. SMITH, and forming a portion of the column under Maj.-Gen. BUTLER. Participating in various affairs previously, at the battle of Drury's Bluff, May 16, 1864, this Regiment distinguished itself for great valor and pertinacity, and won the reputation it has since enjoyed, of being one of the most resolute Regiments in the service. Out of about three hundred and fifty men engaged, it lost in this conflict, in casualties, one hundred and ninety-eight men and thirteen officers, and it is a most noteworthy fact that, having taken two hundred prisoners from the enemy, *the Regiment had considerably more prisoners at the close of the action than it had men fit for duty.* At the important action of Coal Harbor, the Regiment was again engaged, losing seventy men and four officers; again at Petersburgh, where Major PRUYN, then commanding, was killed; at the successful assault on Fort Harrison, Sept. 29th, 1864, where its commanding officer, Colonel NICHOLS, was severely wounded; and at the affair on the Williamsburgh Road, Oct. 27 — in all these actions suffering heavily. At the affair on the Williamsburgh Road, the Regiment, being partially armed with Spencer's Rifles, distinguished itself by its services in skirmishes. Only a few of these weapons being in the possession of the Division, and being distributed unequally among the various Regiments, I ordered them to be collected and issued to this Regiment as being thoroughly competent to use with vigor and efficiency this destructive weapon. With this weapon they will return to your State armed, and it is a most appropriate testimonial of their efficiency."

The Regiment is here represented and its Flags carried by Sergeant POTTER W. KENYON.

COLORS OF THE 119th REGIMENT, N. Y. S. V.

Seven Flags.

---

1. *National Flag*, silk; very little remaining; original staff broken.

2. *Regimental Banner*, blue silk; only a small portion remaining; originally painted with arms of the city of New York, number of Regiment, &c.; original staff.

3. *National Flag*, silk; new; inscribed, "119th Regt., N. Y. S. V."

4, 5. *Guidons*, blue silk; new; inscribed, "N. Y. S. V., 119th Regiment."

6. *National Flag*, silk; new; inscribed, "119th Regt., N. Y. S. V.," and with the names of the following battles: Gettysburg, Wahatchie, Missionary Ridge, Relief of Knoxville, Rocky Faced Ridge, Resaca, Dallas, Pine Hill, Kolb's Farm, Kenesaw, Peach Tree Creek, Atlanta, Savannah, Charleston, Columbia, Bentonville. Presented by the City of New York.

7. *Regimental Banner*, blue silk; new; arms of the State of New York on one side, and of the city of New York on the other. Presented by the City of New York.

The Flags *one* to *five*, were delivered to the mustering out officer at Hart's Island, New York Harbor, June 21, 1865, and by him returned to the Adjutant-General. *Six* and *seven* were returned to the Bureau by Col. J. T. LOCKMAN, who represents them on this occasion. They are carried by Color-Sergeant SCHAFFNER. The new National is inscribed with the names of sixteen battles, sieges and triumphs in which the Regiment participated, from Gettysburg to Raleigh.

The 119th was from New York city, and went out under the command of the late Col. ELIAS PEISSNER, who died of wounds received at Chancellorville.

COLORS OF THE 120th REGIMENT, N. Y. S. V.

One Flag.

1. *National Flag*, silk; with staff.

This Flag was returned to the Adjutant-General on the muster out of the Regiment, June, 1865, without history.

The 120th Regiment was recruited in the counties of Ulster and Greene, under the July and August calls of 1862. It was a part of the famous Sickles' Brigade, and participated in the following battles: Fredericksburgh, Chancellorsville, Gettysburg, Wapping Heights, James City, Strawberry Plains, Mine Run, Kelly's Ford, Raccoon Ford, Wilderness, Spottsylvania, Tolopotomy, North Anna, Coal Harbor, Siege of Petersburgh, Po River, Guinness' Station, Poplar Grove Church, Boydtown Plank Road (two battles), Deep Bottom (two battles), Hatcher's Run, Amelia Springs, and the Surrender of LEE's army.

COLORS OF THE 123d REGIMENT, N. Y. S. V.

Three Flags.

---

1. *National Flag.* silk; end and top ragged; lower and outside upper corner gone; and also about one-eighth of flag farthest from staff; inscribed in needlework, "123d Regt., N. Y. V." Original staff; spear-head gone.

This Flag was presented to the Regiment, by the ladies of Washington county, before leaving for the field in September, 1862. It was used by the Regiment until February, 1865.

2. *National Flag*, silk; original staff.

This Flag was returned to the Adjutant-General on the muster out of the Regiment, June, 1865.

3. *National Garrison Flag*, bunting; used by the Regiment while on garrison duty.

The 123d Regiment was recruited in Washington county, and was mustered into service Sept. 4, 1862. It participated in the following battles: Chancellorsville, Gettysburg, Resaca, Cassville, New Hope Church or Dallas, Pine Mountain, Lost Mountain, Kenesaw Mountain, Kulp's Farm, Chattahoochie River, Peach Tree Creek, Atlanta, Montieth Swamp, Savannah, Columbia, Chesterfield Court House, Averysborough, Bentonville, Moccasin Swamp, Raleigh.

Represented by Gen. JAMES C. ROGERS.

COLORS OF THE 124th REGIMENT, N. Y. S. V.

One Flag.

---

1. *Regimental Banner*, blue silk; with arms and motto of United States, and number of Regiment; original staff, &c.

This Flag was returned to the Adjutant-General on the muster out of the Regiment, June, 1865. It was received by the Regiment from the Quartermaster-General.

The 124th Regiment, sometimes known as the "American Guard," but more generally as the "Orange Blossoms," was recruited in the county of Orange, under the July and August calls of 1862. It was in the following actions: Manassas Gap, 1st Fredericksburgh, Chancellorsville, Beverly Ford, Gettysburg, Wapping Heights, Auburn, Kelly's Ford, Jones' Cross Roads, Mine Run, Wilderness, Po River, Spottsylvania, North Anna, Coal Harbor, Petersburgh, Deep Bottom, Strawberry Plains, Boydtown Road, Hatcher's Run, 25th March, Sailor's Creek, and Surrender of Gen. LEE. The battles of the campaign of 1864–5, thus briefly stated, embraced the actions of May 5, 6, 10, 12, 15, 18, 24, and 30; June 1, 4, 9, 16, 18, and 19; July 30; August 14, 16, and 20; two engagements at Deep Bottom; the siege of Petersburgh, and the final assault on the enemy's works. From the time of entering the service, until the disbandment of the army, it was in active duty, and lost severely in killed and wounded. Its Colonel, A. VAN HORNE ELLIS, and its Major, JAMES CROMWELL, were killed at Gettysburg. Col. CUMMINGS, who succeeded Col. ELLIS, was compelled to resign from wounds; and its Colonel by brevet, Lieut. Col. CHAS. WEYGANT, was several times wounded, and received balls through every article of his clothing. Capts. NICOLL, JACKSON, CRIST, FINNEGAN, and McCORMICK, were killed in battle; Capts. MURRAY, BUSH, BENEDICT, and MAPES, disabled by wounds; and a long list of subordinate officers and privates have fallen under its banners.

The first Color-Bearer of the Regiment was THOMAS FOLEY, who was killed at the battle of Chancellorsville, May 3, 1863. The second was HIRAM KETCHUM, who took the Colors after FOLEY's death, and was wounded in the same battle. The third was WM. H. HAZEN, who carried the Colors until June 7, 1863. The fourth was SAMUEL McQUOID, wounded at Gettysburg, July 2, 1863. No other Color-Bearers were injured. The following Color-Corporals were killed or wounded: W. L. FAIRCHILD, killed at Chancellorsville; ANDREW ARMSTRONG, wounded at Gettysburg; JAMES P. MOULTON, wounded in the Wilderness; AUSTIN LAMOREUX, wounded June 18th, 1864, and again in the assault on Petersburgh, and died of his wounds; JOHN ACKER, who took the Colors on the morning of the 18th of June, and was shot through the head in the afternoon of the same day; ARCHIBALD FREEMAN, wounded May 12th, having previously captured the Colors of the 17th Louisiana; and JOHN SCOTT, killed at Gettysburg.

Two Flags were presented to the Regiment by the ladies of Orange county, and were returned to them.

COLORS OF THE 125th REGIMENT, N. Y. S. V.

Two Flags.

---

1. *Regimental Banner*, blue silk; arms and motto of United States; original staff.
2. *National Flag*, silk; original staff.

These Flags were returned to the Adjutant-General, June, 1865.

The 125th Regiment was recruited in the Twelfth Senatorial District. It was mustered into the service at Troy, August 27, 1862; was sent to Harper's Ferry, and took part in the defense and surrender of that place under Col. MILES. It reëntered the field June 25th, 1863, and was assigned to the 3d Brigade, 3d Division, Second Army Corps. It was in battle at Gettysburg (where it lost 26 killed, 104 wounded, and 9 missing), Auburn Hills, Bristow Station (where it captured a battery of five guns), Blackburn's Ford, Robertson's Tavern, Mine Run, Morton's Ford, Wilderness, Spottsylvania, Po River, North Anna, Coal Harbor, three engagements before Petersburgh, Reams' Station, Hatcher's Run, Southside Railroad, and the pursuit of LEE. It went out with 1,040 men, and returned (June 8, 1865) with 240.

COLORS OF THE 126th REGIMENT, N. Y. S. V.

Two Flags.

---

1. *Regimental Banner*, blue silk; in good condition; arms and motto of United States and number of Regiment; original staff, &c.
2. *National Flag*, silk; faded; inscribed, "Gettysburg, Bristow Station, Mine Run, Wilderness, Po River, Spottsylvania, North Anna, Tolopotomy, Coal Harbor, Petersburgh, Strawberry Plains, Deep Bottom, Reams' Station," and "126th Regiment, N. Y. S. V."

These Flags were returned to the Adjutant-General in June, 1865, and are here carried by Private LEONARD SEITZ.

The 126th Regiment was organized at Geneva, under the calls of July and August, 1862, and was composed of volunteers from the counties of Yates, Seneca, and Ontario, and a few from Monroe. Its first service in the field was at Harper's Ferry, where it shared in the surrender by Col. MILES. It was exchanged and returned to the field in November, 1862, and performed duty as a part of the Third Corps, in the vicinity of Washington, until June, 1863, when it was made a part of the 3d Brigade, 3d Division, Second Army Corps, Army of the Potomac, and remained with that army until its disbandment. At the battle of Gettysburg its fighting career commenced, and there it lost 40 killed, 181 wounded, and 11 missing. Among the killed was Col. SHERRILL and Captains WHEELER, HERENDEEN, and SHIMER; and among the wounded were two Captains and six Lieutenants. One Color-Bearer was shot dead and one severely wounded. It was on the move for thirty-eight days prior to August 1st, 1863; marched 430 miles, laid in line of battle eight days, and fought three days. This baptism of blood and toil it wore with honor in all its subsequent history.

COLORS OF THE 128th REGIMENT, N. Y. S. V.

One Flag.

---

1. *Regimental Banner*, silk; name of Regiment painted on; only a portion remaining; staff gone.

The 128th Regiment was raised in the counties of Duchess and Columbia, during the months of July and August, 1862. It was mustered into the service of the United States September 4th, and left Hudson for Washington on the 5th of that month. It was sent to New Orleans in December, 1862; was in the assault on Port Hudson, May 23d, 1863; was engaged May 27th at Slaughter's House, where the gallant Colonel COWLES fell mortally wounded, and was in the final assault of June 14th. Subsequently it was in service in the important battles of the Shenandoah Valley, under SHERIDAN.

COLORS OF THE 129th REGIMENT, N. Y. S. V.

One Flag.

1. *Regimental Banner*, blue silk; arms and motto of United States, and number of Regiment; staff gone; belt accompanying.

This Flag was returned to the Adjutant-General June, 1865. It was the Flag of the Regiment while acting as Infantry.

The 129th Regiment was organized at Lockport, and left the State, Aug. 23d, 1862. On the 19th December following, it was changed to the 8th Regiment, N. Y. V., Heavy Artillery. (See 8th Artillery.)

COLORS OF THE 130th REGIMENT, N. Y. S. V.

One Flag.

---

1. *Regimental Banner,* blue silk; painted with arms of the United States and motto, and also number of Regiment; original staff.

The 130th Regiment was organized by the Senatorial Committee of the 30th District, at Portage, and was recruited in Livingston, Wyoming and Allegany counties. In the autumn of 1862, it was sent to Fortress Monroe, and was engaged in the operations near Suffolk, as a part of the Seventh Army Corps. On the 11th August, 1863, it was changed to the 19th N. Y. Cavalry; and since September 10th, 1863, it has been known as the First Regiment of Dragoons, N. Y. S. V. These Colors were borne by the Regiment only during its service as an Infantry organization.

COLORS OF THE 131st REGIMENT, N. Y. S. V.

Five Flags.

---

1. *National Flag*, silk; almost entirely destroyed; original staff gone.
2. *Regimental Banner*, blue silk; arms and motto of United States; "131st N. Y. Vol. Regiment, Infantry," in scroll below.
3. *Regimental Banner*, red silk; embroidered with arms of State of New York; "Deus Justus," in scroll; "1st Regt. Metropolitan Guard" and "Excelsior" on and over escutcheon; in scroll below, "As our fathers for us, 1776 — 1862, we for our children."
4. 5. *Guidons*, silk; embroidered with "131st Regt., N. Y. V."

The National (1) and Regimental (2) were received from the General Government. The Regimental Banner (3) and the Guidons (4, 5) were presented by citizens of New York, through HORACE H. DAY, Esq., at Annapolis, Md.

The 131st, or "First Regiment Metropolitan Guard," was recruited in the city of New York, under the auspices of the Metropolitan Police. It was mustered into service Sept. 9th, 1862; was stationed at Annapolis, Md., until Nov. 18, 1862, when it joined the Banks Expedition, and was assigned to the 1st Brigade, 4th Division, Nineteenth Army Corps.

COLORS OF THE 132d REGIMENT, N. Y. S. V.

Four Flags.

---

1. *Regimental Banner*, blue silk; painted with arms of the city of New York, "132d Regiment, N. Y. V. Infantry," and "Presented by the City of New York;" original staff.
2. *National Flag*, silk; inscribed, "Jackson's Mill, N. C., June 21st and 22d, 1864;" "Bachelor's Creek, N. C., February 1st, 1864;" "Southwest Creek, N. C., December 11, 1864;" "Kinston, N. C., March 8th, 9th, and 10th, 1865;" original staff.
3. 4. *Guidons*, bunting.

The Regimental Banner was received by the Regiment while at Bachelor's Creek, May, 1863. The National Flag and Guide Colors were drawn from the Quartermaster-General at Washington, D. C., October 2d, 1862. They are all much worn by service, but not particularly injured in battle, the Color-Bearers having been especially enjoined not to wantonly expose them to the enemy's fire. The lettering (black) on the National Flag, was placed there in the field by a private soldier of the Regiment, who cut the letters from black cloth and sewed them on.

The 132d, or "Second Regiment Empire (SPINOLA's) Brigade," was recruited in part in the cities of New York and Brooklyn, in the summer of 1862, and finally organized by the consolidation with it of 180 men of the 53d Regiment. It left the State, September 27, 1862; served in the Eighteenth

Army Corps until April, 1865, when it was transferred to the Twenty-third Corps. It was engaged in the following battles: Blackwater, Franklin, and Zuni, N. C., 1862; Pollocksville, Street's Ferry, Newbern, White Oak Creek, and Blount's Mills, 1863; Bachelor's Creek, Jackson's Mills, and Southwest Creek, 1864; Kinston, March 8-10, 1865. It was almost continually on outpost duty. From March, 1865, it was on garrison duty at Salisbury, N. C., at which place it was finally relieved from service.

COLORS OF THE 133d REGIMENT, N. Y. S. V.

Five Flags.

---

1. *Regimental Banner*, blue silk; originally embroidered with eagle and flag of United States; "Union," "Constitution," in scroll, and "133d Regiment, N. Y. V.," to which has since been added, "Port Hudson, May 27, June 14, 1863;" "Bisland, April 12, 13, 1863;" "Mansura, May 16, 1864;" original staff, &c.

2. *National Flag*, silk; inscribed with number of Regiment and also with the names of battles; original staff, &c.

3. *Regimental Banner*, blue silk; new; emblazoned with arms of the city of New York; "133d Regiment N. Y. V.," and "Presented by the City of New York."

4. *National Flag*, silk; only a small portion remaining.

5. *Regimental Banner*, blue silk; only a small portion remaining.

The Regimental Banner (No. 1) and the National Flag (No. 2), were presented to the Regiment by Captain MOUNT, of the Metropolitan Police, in behalf of citizens of New York city, September, 1862, at Camp Arthur, Staten Island. They were carried in the battles of Bisland, La., April 12, 13, 1863; Port Hudson, May 23 to July 8, 1863 (including two grand assaults, May 27 and June 14); skirmishes at Vermilion Bayou, La., and Carrion Crow Bayou, La.; battle of Mansura Plains, La.; skirmish at Snicker's Ford, Va., July, 1864, and battle of Cedar Creek, Va., October 19, 1864. Flags 3, 4 and

5 were returned to the Adjutant-General on the muster out of the Regiment, June, 1865.

The 133d, or "Second Regiment Metropolitan Guard," was recruited under the auspices of the Metropolitan Police. It was in service in the Louisiana campaigns of 1863–4, and subsequently under SHERIDAN in the Valley of the Shenandoah.

COLORS OF THE 134th REGIMENT, N. Y. S. V.

Two Flags.

---

1. *Regimental Banner*, blue silk; arms and motto of United States, and number of Regiment; original staff.
2. *National Flag*, silk; original staff.

These Flags were returned to the Adjutant-General, without history.

The 134th Regiment was recruited in the counties of Delaware, Schoharie and Schenectady, and was mustered into the United States service on the 22d of September, 1862, at Schoharie C. H. It joined Gen. SIGEL's Corps (the 11th) at Fairfax C. H., about the 2d of October following, and served with that Corps during the battles of Chancellorsville and Gettysburg. In September, 1863, it left for Tennessee as a part of the Twentieth Corps under General HOOKER, and assisted in opening the "cracker line" through Lookout Valley to ROSECRANS' army. It lay in that valley until the battles of Lookout Mountain and Missionary Ridge, in which latter engagement the Regiment participated in the charge and drove the enemy from their works. It then moved to the relief of Knoxville, assisted in raising the siege and then returned to Lookout Valley. During this march, in common with other Regiments, it suffered terribly, having moved on a "dog trot" all the way with nothing to eat but a little flour and pork captured from the enemy. It came back fatigued and in rags. It remained in Lookout Valley until May 4th, 1864, when it broke camp and started on the memorable Atlanta campaign. It was in every battle on this march, the principal of which were Rocky Faced Ridge, Resaca, Dallas, Pine Knob, Lost Mountain, and Peach Tree Creek, and entered Atlanta Sept. 3d. It garrisoned that city while HOOD was being driven North, and on the 15th November started on the Savannah campaign. It entered Savannah on the 21st December, and remained until the 27th January, 1865, when it started on the march through South Carolina, crossed almost impassable swamps, and arrived at Goldsboro, N. C. It afterwards moved to Raleigh and remained in that section until the surrender of General JOHNSTON, when it marched to Washington and took part in the grand review of SHERMAN'S Army. It was mustered out of service on the 10th of June.

COLORS OF THE 135th REGIMENT, N. Y. S. V.

One Flag.

---

1. *Regimental Banner*, blue silk; emblazoned with arms of United States and motto, and "135th N. Y. Vol. Regiment, Infantry."

The 135th Regiment, or "Anthony Wayne Guard," was recruited in the Eighth Senatorial District (composed of the counties of Westchester, Putnam and Rockland), and was mustered into the service of the United States, Sept. 2d, 1862. By order of the Secretary of War (Oct. 3, 1862), it was transferred from the Infantry to the Artillery arm of the service, and designated as the "Sixth Regiment, New York State Artillery." The Flag presented was received from the General Government, and was carried by the Regiment during its service as Infantry.

COLORS OF THE 136th REGIMENT, N. Y. S. V.

Four Flags.

---

1. *National Flag*, silk; worn; with staff.
2. *National Flag*, silk; new; inscribed, "Chancellorsville, Gettysburg, Lookout Mountain, Chattanooga, Missionary Ridge, Knoxville, Buzzard's Roost Gap, Resaca, Cassville, Dallas, Gilgal Church, Kulp's Farm, Kenesaw Mountain, Peach Tree Creek, Turner's Ferry, Atlanta, Milledgeville, Savannah, Charleston, Averysburgh, Bentonville, Goldsboro, Raleigh."
3. 4. *Guidons*, silk; with staffs.

These Flags were returned to the Adjutant-General in June. The old National was in all the engagements in which the Regiment took part from Chattanooga to Raleigh. The new National was obtained from the War Department, and was inscribed, by the direction of Col. WOOD, with the names of the battles in which the Regiment was engaged.

The 136th Regiment was organized at Portage Falls, N. Y., and mustered into service September 25th, 1862. It was composed of five companies from Livingston county, two from Allegany, and three from Wyoming. On the 10th of October, 1862, it was assigned to the Eleventh Corps under General SIGEL, and participated in the movements of that Corps until the 14th April, 1864, when it became a part of the 3d Brigade, 3d Division, Twentieth Corps.

COLORS OF THE 137th REGIMENT, N. Y. S. V.

One Flag.

---

1. *National Flag*, silk; much worn; with staff.

This Flag was returned to the Adjutant-General.

The 137th Regiment was mustered into service at Binghamton in September, 1862. It was recruited in the counties of Cortland, Broome and Tioga. It was attached to the 3d Brigade, 2d Division (White Star), Twelfth Army Corps, at Harper's Ferry, Oct., 1862, and remained in that command until the organization of the Twentieth Corps (by the consolidation of the Eleventh and Twelfth), April, 1864. It was in the Chancellorsville and Gettysburg campaigns, and in the battles and marches of SHERMAN's army from Lookout Mountain to Raleigh.

COLORS OF THE 139th REGIMENT, N. Y. S. V.

Five Flags.

---

1. *National Flag*, silk; with staff.
2. *Regimental Banner*, blue silk; arms and motto of United States and number of Regiment; staff, &c.
3, 4. *Guidons*, silk; "139" in center.
5. *National Flag*, silk.

These Flags were received by the Adjutant-General, in June. They are here represented by Brevet Brig.-Gen. ROBERTS. The National Flag (5) was carried in fifteen engagements, including Drury's Bluff, Coal Harbor, Petersburgh, Fair Oaks, Fort Harrison, &c., and was one of the first to enter Richmond. It is here borne by Color-Bearer GEORGE W. SMITH, who was wounded while carrying it in the assault and capture of Fort Harrison, Sept. 29, 1864.

The 139th Regiment was recruited on Long Island, and was organized at Brooklyn in August, 1862. It served in Virginia and North Carolina.

COLORS OF THE 140th REGIMENT, N. Y. S. V.

Three Flags.

---

1. *National Flag*, silk; almost entirely destroyed; with staff.
2. *Regimental Banner*, blue silk; on one side "God help the Right," arms and motto of the United States, and "140th Regt., N. Y. S. V.;" on the other, "Presented by 34 Young Ladies of Rochester, N. Y., to the Monroe County Regiment," and arms and motto of the State of New York; original staff, &c.
3. *Regimental Banner*, blue silk; arms and motto of United States and number of Regiment; original staff.

These Flags were returned to the Adjutant-General.

The 140th Regiment was recruited in Rochester, N. Y., in twelve days. It was organized Sept. 1, and mustered in Sept. 13, 1862. It was assigned to the 1st Brigade, 2d Division, Fifth Army Corps. It was in actions at Snicker's Gap, Fredericksburgh, Chancellorsville, Gettysburg, Beverly Ford, Mine Run, Wilderness, Robertson's Tavern, Spottsylvania, North Anna, Coal Harbor, Petersburgh, Weldon Railroad, and in all the actions in which the Fifth Corps took part. Cols. O'RORKE and RYAN, Lieut.-Col. RANDALL, Major STARKS, and other officers fell in battle.

COLORS OF THE 141st REGIMENT, N. Y. S. V.

One Flag.

---

1. *National Flag*, silk; with staff.

This Flag was returned to the Adjutant-General.

The 141st Regiment was organized at Elmira under the July and August calls of 1862, and left the State on the 15th September of that year. It was in service at Suffolk, Va., and on the Peninsula until July, 1863, when it was assigned to the Eleventh Corps, and accompanied it to Tennessee. By subsequent consolidation of the Eleventh and Twelfth Corps it became part of the Twentieth Corps, in which it remained until the disbandment of the army. It was engaged in the battles of Missionary Ridge, Lookout Mountain, Relief of Knoxville, Resaca, Dallas, Atlanta, Kenesaw, Peach Tree Creek, and the subsequent movements of SHERMAN's army from Atlanta to Raleigh.

COLORS OF THE 143d REGIMENT, N. Y. S. V.

Two Flags.

---

1. *Regimental Banner*, silk; embroidered on both sides with the State motto and military arms, and the words "Sullivan County," also, the words, "Presented by the citizens of Sullivan county, Oct., 1862;" original staff, and belt of Color-Bearer.

2. *National Flag*, silk; worn; inscribed as follows: "Nansemond, May 30, 1863; Lookout Valley, Oct. 28 and 29, 1863; Chattanooga, Nov. 23, 24, 25, 1863; Relief of Knoxville, November 29 to December 16, 1863."

These Flags (in addition to the engagements inscribed upon them) have been borne by the Regiment through as many States as formed the Union in 1776.

The 143d Regiment was recruited in Sullivan county in August and September, 1862, and was mustered into service Oct. 8 and 9 of that year. It has taken part in the following engagements, viz.: Nansemond, Lookout Valley (two), Chattanooga (three), Relief of Knoxville (two), Resaca, Dallas, Kenesaw Mountain, Peach Tree Ridge, and Atlanta. It shared in the march under Gen. SHERMAN from Atlanta to Savannah, and the subsequent movements of that command.

COLORS OF THE 146th REGIMENT, N. Y. S. V.

One Flag.

---

1. *Regimental Banner*, blue silk; painted with arms of United States and motto, and inscribed "Halleck Infantry," "146th N. Y. Vol. Regiment Infantry;" original spear and cord and tassels; staff gone.

This Flag was carried by the Regiment in the campaigns of 1862–3.

The 146th Regiment was organized at Rome, under the direction of the Senatorial Committee of the 19th District, and left the State September 27, 1862. It has been frequently designated the "Fifth Oneida," but its original synonym was "Halleck Infantry," in honor of Gen. HALLECK, whose birth-place was in the county where it was raised. It was engaged in the battles of Fredericksburgh, Chancellorsville, Gettysburg, Rappahannock Station, Bristow Station, Mine Run, Williamsport, Wapping Heights, Wilderness, Spottsylvania, Laurel Hill, North Anna, Tolopotomy, Bethesda Church, Petersburgh, Weldon Railroad, Chapel House, Hatcher's Run (two), Hicks' Ford, White Oak Road, Five Forks, Appomattox C. H., LEE's Surrender. It lost two field officers and four line officers, killed in battle; two by disease, five by resignation on account of wounds, and one by transfer. Sixteen of its officers and five hundred and twenty-five of its enlisted men were wounded in battle. One hundred and sixty-two of its enlisted men were killed in battle, one hundred and five died of disease, five hundred and fifty were discharged for wounds and disability, three hundred and twenty-four were transferred, and four hundred and twenty-seven mustered out of service.

COLORS OF THE 147th REGIMENT, N. Y. S. V.

Three Flags.

1. *National Flag*, silk; original staff.
2, 3. *Guidons*, silk; staffs gone.

These Flags were drawn from the General Government in March, 1864, and were returned to the Adjutant-General on the muster out of the Regiment in June, 1865. They were carried in the following actions, viz.: Wilderness, Spottsylvania, Coal Harbor, Petersburgh, Pettle's Farm, Hatcher's Run, Dabney's Mills, Gravelly Run, Laurel Hill, North Anna, Bottom's Bridge, Weldon Railroad, Chapel House, Bellfield, Five Forks, and LEE's Surrender.

The 147th was recruited in Oswego county, in the summer and fall of 1862. It took part in the Chancellorsville and Gettysburg campaigns, and in the campaigns under Gen. GRANT in 1864–5.

COLORS OF THE 148th REGIMENT, N. Y. S. V.

One Flag.

---

1. *Regimental Banner*, silk; outside end of flag ragged and fringe gone; staff broken near spear-head; eagle with National motto in scroll; stars in field over the eagle. Inscribed "148th N. Y. Vol. Regiment Infantry," in scroll beneath. No history accompanying.

The 148th Regiment was organized at Geneva, in the autumn of 1862, and left for Washington in September. It was composed of companies from Seneca, Yates and Ontario counties. It was on garrison and provost duty until the campaign of 1864, when it was sent to the field and was engaged in the siege of Petersburgh, the battle of Drury's Bluff, the battle of Coal Harbor, and others.

COLORS OF THE 150th REGIMENT, N. Y. S. V.

Two Flags.

---

1. *Regimental Banner*, blue silk; arms and motto of United States, and "150th N. Y. Vol. Regiment Infantry;" original staff.

2. *National Flag*, silk; in tatters; original staff; spear gone.

These Flags were returned to the Adjutant-General, on the muster out of the Regiment in June last.

The 150th Regiment was recruited in the counties of Duchess and Columbia, and organized at Poughkeepsie in Oct., 1862. It was in the campaigns of Gettysburg and Atlanta, and from Atlanta to Savannah and Raleigh, N. C.

COLORS OF THE 151st REGIMENT, N. Y. S. V.

Five Flags.

---

1. *Regimental Banner*, with United States arms and motto painted upon each side.
2. *National Flag*, silk; four-fifths gone.

These Flags were received by the Regiment, from the State, about the 1st of October, 1862. They were borne in the following engagements, viz.: Wapping Heights, McLane's Ford, Kelly's Ford, Locust Grove, and Mine Run. At Locust Grove the Color-Bearer, Sergt. H. E. EARL, Jr., was wounded three times.

3. *National Flag*, silk; with staff.
4. 5. *Guidons*.

These Flags were returned to the Adjutant-General, without history.

The 151st Regiment was organized in the 29th Senatorial District, and was composed of companies from the counties of Niagara, Genesee and Ontario.

COLORS OF THE 153d REGIMENT, N. Y. S. V.

Three Flags.

---

1. *Regimental Banner*, blue silk; with arms and motto of United States, and "153d N. Y. Vol. Regiment Infantry."
2. 3. *Guidons*, white silk; "153" in center; without staffs.

The Guidons were presented to the Regiment by Mrs. JOSEPH STRAIN, Albany, N. Y., Nov., 1862. They were carried on the Red River Expedition, and were in the battles and skirmishes at Sabine Cross Roads, Pleasant Hill, Marksville, Cane River Crossing, and Alexandria, La.

The 153d Regiment was recruited principally in Montgomery, Clinton, Essex and Fulton counties, in the fall of 1862. It was on guard and police duty in the vicinity of Washington until Feb., 1864, when it was sent to New Orleans, and, as part of the 1st Brigade, 1st Division, Nineteenth Army Corps, was engaged at Sabine Cross Roads, Pleasant Hill, Cane River and Mansura. It returned to Washington in July, 1864, and served in the Shenandoah Valley campaign under General SHERIDAN.

Represented by Lieut.-Col. ALEX. STRAIN.

COLORS OF THE 156th REGIMENT, N. Y. S. V.

One Flag.

---

1. *National Flag*, silk; without staff.

This Flag was furnished to the Regiment by the State; about three-fifths of the Flag is gone; the union and the stars and stripes below the union remaining. It was gallantly borne in the engagements at Bisland and at Port Hudson, La.

The 156th Regiment was organized at Kingston, Ulster county, N. Y., under the synonym of "The Mountain Legion." It was mustered into the service of the United States, Nov. 17, 1862, and left the State for New Orleans, Dec. 4th of that year. It served with credit in the campaign terminating in the capture of Port Hudson. It performed provost duty at Baton Rouge during the winter of 1863–4, and in the spring was engaged in the Red River expedition under Gen. BANKS. It returned to Washington with the Nineteenth Army Corps, in the spring of 1864, and served with credit under General SHERIDAN at Opequan, Fisher's Hill, and Cedar Creek. By order of the Corps Commander, the names of Bisland, Port Hudson, Mansura, Opequan, Fisher's Hill, and Cedar Creek, were inscribed on the Banner of the Regiment.

COLORS OF THE 157th REGIMENT, N. Y. S. V.

One Flag.

1. *National Flag*, silk; with staff.

Returned to the Adjutant-General, without history.

The 157th Regiment was organized at Hamilton, N. Y., and was mustered into service September 19, 1862. It was composed of five companies recruited in Madison county, and five companies recruited in Cortland county. It was first assigned to a Provisional Brigade, and subsequently to the 1st Brigade, 3d Division, Eleventh Army Corps. In August, 1863, it was transferred, with the 1st Division, Eleventh Corps, to the Department of the South. It was in the battles of Chancellorsville, Gettysburg, Fort Wagner, John's Island (two), Honey Hill, S. C., and Dingle's Mill. At Chancellorsville, the 157th N. Y., and the 61st Ohio, were the only Regiments of the Eleventh Corps that stood their ground and retired in good order at the word of command. At Dingle's Mill, S. C., it had the honor of driving the enemy from a strongly intrenched position, and of capturing two pieces of artillery, one battle-flag and many prisoners.

COLORS OF THE 162d REGIMENT, N. Y. S. V.

Two Flags.

---

1. *National Flag*, silk; union torn out by charge of grape.
2. *Regimental Banner*, blue silk; in the center of which is painted the national coat of arms.

These Flags were presented to the Regiment, October 18, 1862. They were borne at Bisland and Port Hudson, La. At the latter place the union was torn from the National Flag by a charge of grape shot. In the Red River campaign, the Colors were present in the following engagements, viz.: Sabine Cross Roads, Pleasant Hill (where Col. LEWIS BENEDICT, commanding Brigade, was killed) and Cane River Crossing. Four times have these Colors been shot down in battle; two of their bearers have been killed and two wounded.

The 162d Regiment was organized in the city of New York, in the fall of 1862, under the synonym of the " Third Metropolitan Guard.'

COLORS OF THE 168th REGIMENT, N. Y. S. V.

Two Flags.

---

1. *National Flag*, silk; in good condition.
2. *Regimental Banner*, blue silk; with arms and motto of United States, and "168th N. Y. Vol. Regiment, Infantry."

These Flags were furnished to the Regiment by the Federal Government. The Regiment was organized at Newburgh. Orange county, in the fall of 1862, for nine months' service, It was composed of men recruited in Orange, Westchester and Broome counties. It was principally engaged in guard duty at Baltimore and Norfolk, Va.

COLORS OF THE 169th REGIMENT, N. Y. S. V.

Two Flags.

1. *National Flag*, silk.
2. *Regimental Banner*, silk.

These Flags were presented to the Regiment by the State in September, 1862. They are injured in every part. Each has at least one hundred holes from bullets and shell, and the holes have now run into each other and appear like rents. The staff of the Regimental Banner was so shattered by bullets as to be useless, and was replaced by a staff captured from the enemy near Petersburgh at the time of the mine explosion. Ten different Bearers have been killed or wounded while carrying these Colors. They have been in the following engagements, viz.: Edenton Road, Carrsville, Blackwater Ford, Blackwater Bridge, Zuni, Nansemond or Providence Church, South Anna, Siege of Forts Wagner and Gregg, Rantoul Bridge, Cedar Creek or King's Road, Walthall Junction, Chester Station, Drury's Bluff, Foster's Plantation (two), Coal Harbor, Petersburgh (three), Dutch Gap, 2d Malvern Hill, and Chapin's Farm or Fort Harrison; also in several brisk skirmishes.

The 169th Regiment was organized at Troy, N. Y., under command of Col. CLARENCE BUEL, and was mustered into service Oct. 6, 1862. In addition to the engagements in which the Flags here presented have been under fire, it has participated in the following, viz.: Darbytown Road, Oct. 7, 1864; Fort Fisher, Dec. 25, 1864; and Fort Fisher, Jan. 15, 1865; on which last occasion it was the first to reach the shore, and, in the explosion of the magazine of the Fort, suffered severely — one hundred and twenty-seven enlisted men and thirteen officers being killed or wounded. Col. BUEL was the first person belonging to the Regiment who was wounded. Col. JOHN McCONIHE, his successor in command, was killed at Coal Harbor; and Colonel (now Brevet Brig.-Gen.) ALONZO ALDEN was blown up by the explosion of the Fort Fisher magazine and seriously injured.

COLORS OF THE 176th REGIMENT, N. Y. S. V.

Two Flags.

---

1. *National Flag*, silk.
2. *Regimental Banner*, silk.

These Flags were furnished to the Regiment at New Orleans, La., on the 4th of July, 1863, by the Quartermaster Department of the Department of the Gulf, to replace colors captured by the rebels and since recaptured. There is very little of the Flags remaining. The staff of the Regimental Banner was lost at Cedar Creek, Va., where the Color-Bearer, Sergeant ALBERT GHERKIN, was killed. A portion of the Flag was saved by the members of the Color-Guard, and both colors placed upon one staff. They were carried by the Regiment during the Red River campaign, in the spring of 1864; in Gen. SHERIDAN'S campaign in the Shenandoah Valley, Va., in the summer and fall of the same year, and during the service of the Regiment in Georgia and North Carolina in the winter and spring of 1865. They were under fire at Mansura, La., May 16, 1864, at Opequan, Va., Sept. 19, 1864, at Fisher's Hill, Va., Sept. 22, 1864, and at Cedar Creek, Oct. 19, 1864. At Opequan, Va., three of the Color-Guard were wounded; at Fisher's Hill one was killed, and at Cedar Creek, the bearer of the Regimental Banner was killed, and one of the guard wounded. The National Color was borne in all actions by Color-Sergeant LUKE B. CASEY, who always proved himself worthy of the trust. At Fisher's Hill, these Colors were the first of the Nineteenth Corps that were carried into the enemy's trenches, and the Regiment captured four pieces of artillery. At Cedar Creek, although the Regiment was the first of the Nineteenth Corps to be attacked, these Colors were the last to leave the trenches when the Corps was, for a time, compelled to retreat. These facts, which are communicated by CHAS. LEWIS, Major commanding, are fully sustained by official report.

The 176th, or "Ironsides" Regiment, was organized at Brooklyn in Dec., 1862, having received, by consolidation, two hundred and seventy-two men recruited in Orange county for the 166th Regiment, and a number recruited for the 52d National Guard in Brooklyn. It served as a part of the Nineteenth Corps, from July 20, 1864, to April 10, 1865, and is now a part of the Tenth Corps.

COLORS OF THE 177th REGIMENT, N. Y. S. V. 10th N. Y. S. N. G.

Two Flags.

---

1. *National Flag*, silk; torn; original staff in part. Presented to the Regiment at Bonné Carré, La., by Mrs. Lieut. EDWARD H. MERRIHEW, of Albany, N. Y.

2. *Regimental Banner*, blue silk; painted with arms of United States and motto, and number of Regiment.

The 10th Regiment National Guard was organized at Albany, under Col. IRA W. AINSWORTH, soon after the breaking out of the rebellion, and performed guard duty and other service, in aid of the General Government, by order of Gov. MORGAN. Under a special order of the War Department accepting volunteers for nine months, it tendered its services for the third time to Gov. MORGAN. In September, 1862, it was accepted and assigned to Gen. BANKS, under the name of the 177th Volunteers, and sailed with the expedition in December, for the Department of the Gulf.

On its arrival at New Orleans, it was attached to the Third Brigade, Second Division, Nineteenth Corps, and served in holding the defenses of New Orleans until March, when the campaign of Louisiana was commenced. It served with the Brigade in two campaigns on the Amite river, each time being sharply engaged by the enemy, and lost its first man in action. It then participated in the campaigns from New Orleans to Port Hudson, and arrived in front of the enemy's works on the 23d of May. On the 25th, Gen. BANKS, wishing to ascertain the position of the enemy, and to open communication with the fleet, ordered the Regiment to cut its way through to the river. This service was gallantly performed under a heavy fire from the enemy's main works. The Regiment approached so close to the fortifications that the guns of the forts over-ranged, thus saving the Regiment from great loss in killed and wounded. The first blood at Port Hudson was drawn from the 177th on this reconnoisance.

The Regiment was actively engaged during the entire siege of Port Hudson, taking part in the battles of May 27th and June 14th. It also served as the supporting column in the hand grenade assault on the citadel, on the nights of June 27th and 29th, and suffered severely. On the fall of Port Hudson, the time of the Regiment having expired, it returned home by way of the Mississippi river, the route originally promised by Gen. BANKS to the troops of his expedition. After being mustered out of the United States service, it resumed its original position in the Ninth Brigade, National Guard.

COLORS OF THE 179th REGIMENT, N. Y. S. V.

Four Flags.

---

1. *National Flag*, silk; nearly new; inscribed, "Petersburgh, June 17th and July 30th, 1864; Weldon Railroad; Poplar Spring Church; Hatcher's Run; Petersburgh, April 1st and 2d, 1865."

2. *Regimental Banner*, blue silk; arms and motto of United States and number of Regiment; original staff.

3, 4. *Guidons;* inscribed "179th Regt., N. Y. Vols."

These Flags were returned to the Adjutant-General, without history.

The 179th Regiment was organized at Elmira in 1864, from companies recruited in different parts of the State. It was principally composed of veterans, and hence was put in active service. It was in some of the most important battles of the closing period of the war, as the inscriptions on its Flag indicates.

COLORS OF THE 186th REGIMENT, N. Y. S. V.

Two Flags.

---

1. *Regimental Banner*, blue silk; arms and motto of United States, and number of Regiment; original staff.
2. *National Flag*, silk; original staff gone.

These Flags were returned to the Adjutant General, without history.

The 186th Regiment was recruited principally in Lewis and Jefferson counties, and was mustered into service, Sept. 8th, 1864. It went out 980 strong, lost 130 in killed and wounded, 120 by disease and discharge, and returned with 730. It was in battle of South Side Railroad, Oct. 27, 1864; formed part of WARREN'S command in his raid to Nottaway, Dec. 10; was in the charge on Fort Mahone in front of Petersburgh, April 2, 1865; and then joined in the pursuit and capture of Gen. LEE. It was among the first to enter the rebel fortifications at Petersburgh, and was highly complimented by its Brigade and Division commanders for the gallantry shown in its charge on "Fort Mahone."

COLORS OF THE 189th REGIMENT, N. Y. S. V.

Two Flags.

---

1. *National Flag*, silk; faded; original staff.
2. *Regimental Banner*, blue silk; original staff.

These Flags were returned to the Adjutant-General, without history.

The 189th Regiment was organized at Elmira, Oct. 3, 1864, and was composed of companies recruited in different parts of the State.

COLORS OF THE 1st REGIMENT ARTILLERY, N. Y. S. V.

Two Flags.

1. *Guidon*, of Battery M.
2. *Guidon*, of Battery K.

These Flags were returned to the Adjutant-General without history.

Battery K was organized at Fort Plain, N. Y., in September, 1861, and was known as the Fort Plain Battery. It was mustered at Elmira, Oct. 4, 1861 — LORENZO CROUNSE, Captain; SOLON W. STOCKING, 1st Lieut.; ANGELL MATTHEWSON, 2d Lieut. It was in battles as follows: Harper's Ferry, Cedar Mountain, Beverly Ford, Rappahannock Station, Chantilly, 1st Fredericksburgh, Chancellorsville, Gettysburg, and Mine Run; was in the defenses of Washington from April 1, 1864, until muster out of service.

Battery M was organized in October, 1861, at Lockport, N. Y., under command of Capt. COTHRAN. It was known as "Cothran's Battery," and was in service in the campaign under Gen. SHERMAN.

COLORS OF THE 2d REGIMENT ARTILLERY, N. Y. S. V.

Three Flags.

---

1. *National Flag*, silk; much worn.
2. *Regimental Banner*, yellow silk; design, cannon crossed in center, with name of Regiment; much worn; original staff gone.
3. *National Flag*, silk; small, with the letters "N. Y. S. V.," embroidered; original staff gone.

This Regiment was organized on Staten Island, in 1861, and was known as the "Morgan Artillery." It participated in the following engagements: 2d Bull Run, Aug. 30, 1862; Nye, May 19, 1864; North Anna, May 23 and 26; Tolopotomy, May 31; Coal Harbor, June 2 to 12; Petersburgh, June 16 to 21; Williams' Farm, June 21 to 30; Deep Bottom, July 29; New Market Road, August 14; Charles City Cross Roads, August 17; Reams' Station, August 25. It lost 841 in killed, wounded and missing. Major GEORGE S. DAWSON, of Albany, is among its heroic dead.

COLORS OF 3d ARTILLERY, FORMERLY 19th REGT., N. Y. S. V.

Two Flags.

---

1. *National Flag*, silk.

This Flag is inscribed, by authority, with the names of battles in which it was carried, viz.: Lovettsville, August 18, 1861; Fort Macon, April 26, 1862; Washington, Sept. 6, 1862; Rawle's Mills, Nov. 2, 1862; Southwest Creek, Dec. 13, 1862; Kinston, Dec. 14, 1862; Whitehall, Dec. 16, 1862; Goldsboro, Dec. 17, 1862; Newbern, March 14, 1863; Washington, April, 1863.

2. *National Flag*, silk; inscribed with name of Battery in black letters.

This was the Flag of "Howell's Battery," Co. M, 3d Artillery. This Battery was originally organized in Albany. It was reorganized, as a veteran command, on the first of January, 1864. It served in Virginia and North Carolina; was engaged in thirty-eight regular engagements, and was one hundred consecutive days under the enemy's fire.

The 3d Artillery was organized in the spring of 1861, as the 19th N. Y. S. V. Infantry. It was changed, December 11, 1861, to 3d N. Y. S. V. Artillery. It was known by the synonyms of "Seward Infantry," "Cayuga Regiment," and "Seward Artillery." It was organized at Elmira, and was originally composed of six companies from Auburn, one from

Seneca Falls, one from Moravia, one from Weedsport, and one from Union Springs. Five new companies were added to it in the winter of 1861–2, and one in March, 1862. Four new companies were added in 1863–4, giving a total of men on its rolls, of 4,408. In May, 1863, 532 men were mustered out by expiration of period of enlistment. It lost 217 killed in action; 233 wounded, 247 died, and 355 deserted. The following is a list of the engagements in which the Regiment, or some of its batteries, participated: Martinsburgh, Va., June 11, 1861; Lovettsville, Va., June 11, 1861; Fort Macon, N. C., April 25, 1862; Washington, N. C., Sept. 6, 1862; Rawle's Mills, N. C., Nov. 5, 1862; Southwest Creek, N. C., Dec. 13, 1862; Kinston, N. C., Dec. 14, 1862; Whitehall, N. C., Dec. 16, 1862; Goldsboro, N. C., Dec. 17, 1862; Springbank, N. C., Dec. 17, 1862; Newbern, N. C., March 14, 1863; Deep Gully, N. C., May 13, 1863; Blount's Creek, N. C., April 9, 1863; Gum Swamp, N. C., May, 1863; Cove Creek, N. C., May, 1863; Bachelor's Creek, N. C., May, 1863; Seabrook Island, S. C., June, 1863; Bombardment of Fort Sumter, July 10, 1863; Fort Wagner, S. C., July 18, 1863; Siege of Fort Wagner, July 18, to Sept. 5, 1863; Morris Island, S. C., Aug. 22 to 30, 1863; Camden Court House, Va., Nov. 3, 1863; Dismal Swamp, Va., Nov. 3, 1863; Bombardment of Fort Sumter, Nov. 2 to 5, 1863; Newbern, N. C., Feb. 1 to 4, 1864; Bachelor's Creek, N. C., Feb. 1, 1864; Beech Grove, N. C., Feb. 2, 1864; Brice's Creek, N. C., Feb. 2, 1864; Folly Island, S. C., Feb. 9, 10 and 11, 1864; Fort Clifton, Va., May 9, 1864; Harrison's Church, Va., May 11, 1864; Drury's Bluff, Va., May 13, 14, 15, 16, 1864; Harrison's Plantation, Va., May 15, 1864; Springfield, Va., May 18, 1864; Fort Powhattan, Va., May 21, 1864; Wilson's Wharf,

Va., May 24, 1864; Siege of Petersburgh, Va., to taking of Petersburgh; Petersburgh, Va., June 16, 1864; Walthall Farm, Va., 1864; Friends' Fields, Va., 1864; Chapin's Farm, Va., Sept. 29 and 30, 1864; Fort Harrison, Va., Sept. 29 and 30, 1864; Fort Burnham, Va., Oct. 2, 1864; Fort Harrison, Va., Oct. 7, 1864; Ironclads, James River, Oct. 22, 1864; Honey Hill, S. C., Nov. 30, 1864; Devereaux Neck, S. C., Dec. 7, 1864; Camp Halley, Va., Dec. 10, 1864; Gardner's Bridge, N. C., Dec. 9, 1864; Foster's Mills, N. C., Dec. 10, 1864; Butler's Bridge, N. C., Dec. 12, 1864; Wise's Forks, N. C., March 7, 8, 9, 10, 1864; Richmond, Va., April, 5, 1865; Plymouth Siege, N. C., April 20, 1864; Tarboro, N. C., July, 1863; Ruffin's Farm, Va., 1864; Siege of Charleston, S. C., 1863; John's Island, S. C., 1864; James' Island, S. C. 1864; South Mills, Va., ———; Pocataligo, S. C., 1864. Total, 61.

COLORS OF THE 7th REGIMENT ARTILLERY, N. Y. S. V.

Two Flags.

---

1. *Regimental Banner*, yellow silk; cannon crossed in center; inscribed, "U. S;" "7th N. Y. Vol. Regiment Artillery;" original staff; spear-head gone.
2. *National Flag*, silk; almost entirely destroyed; original staff; spear-head gone.

These Flags were returned to the Adjutant-General, in accordance with general orders of War Department, June, 1865. Out of nine Colors that were in the Brigade in the charge of June 16, 1864, the National Color (2) was the only one that returned. In that charge the Brigade commander was wounded; the next in command was taken prisoner, and Col. HASTINGS, who succeeded to the command, directed the Colors of the 7th to be brought out. One of its bearers was killed and two were wounded in the charge.

The 7th Artillery was organized in the city of Albany in 1862, as the 113th Infantry. It was mustered into service August 18, 1862, and on the 17th of December, of the same year, was changed from Infantry to Heavy Artillery. It was on garrison duty in the vicinity of Washington, until the 15th of May, 1864, when it was sent to the field, as Infantry, as a part of the 2d Division, Second Army Corps. From that time up to the last of February, 1865, it was in all the marches and battles of the Army of the Potomac, as follows:

Spottsylvania Court House, Wilderness, Milford Station, North Anna River, Tolopotomy Creek, Coal Harbor, Petersburgh the 16th, 17th and 22d, and during the whole siege, Deep Bottom (two engagements in July and August), and Reams' Station. It was recalled from the field February 22, 1865, and has since been on garrison duty at Baltimore. Three hundred and eighty-one officers and men (volunteers of 1862) have been mustered out. Three hundred and twenty-two (recruits) were left on duty. Col. LEWIS O. MORRIS, under whom the regiment took the field, was killed by a sharpshooter, at Coal Harbor, on the 4th of June, 1864.

Represented by Col. HASTINGS, of Regiment, and Major ANABLE, of Battalion.

COLORS OF THE 8th REGIMENT ARTILLERY, N. Y. S. V.

One Flag.

---

1. *National Flag*, silk; inscribed, "Spottsylvania, North Anna, Tolopotomy, Coal Harbor, Petersburgh, Strawberry Plains, Deep Bottom, Reams' Station, Boydtown Road, Hatcher's Run, LEE'S Surrender."

These Flags were returned to the Adjutant-General, without history.

The 129th Infantry was recruited under the auspices of Col. PETER A. PORTER, whose wealth, influence, and untiring energy were freely given to the work. It was composed of four companies from Niagara, three from Orleans, and three from Genesee, and was mustered into service at Lockport, August 22, 1862. On the 17th December, 1862, it was changed, by order of the War Department, from Infantry to Heavy Artillery, and designated as the 8th Regiment N. Y. V. Heavy Artillery. It was assigned to the 2d Brigade, Eighth Army Corps, and remained in Baltimore, garrisoning Forts Federal Hill, McHenry and Marshall, until May 16, 1864, with the exception of duty on Maryland Heights, from July 10 to August 3, 1863, and for a short time at Green Spring Run and Romney, in February, 1865. During this time it had raised recruits sufficient to bring the regimental number to 1,923. It was then (May 18, 1864) assigned to the 4th Brigade, 2d Division, Second

Army corps, as Infantry. In this capacity it was engaged in the battles inscribed upon its Flag. Its gallant commander, Col. PORTER, gave his life to his country in the battle of June 3, 1864.

COLORS OF THE 7th INDEPENDENT BATTERY, N. Y. S. V.

One Flag.

---

1. *Guidon*, silk; was torn from staff by a shell at Fair Oaks, and staff broken.

The 7th Battery was raised in Newburgh and Cornwall, under Captain PETER C. REGAN, and originally formed a part of the "Tenth Legion," or 56th Regiment, N. Y. S. V., from which it was detached and made an Independent Battery. It served on the Peninsula, with the Seventh Army Corps, in southeastern Virginia, and subsequently in the movements culminating in the capture of Richmond and Petersburgh, and the surrender of General LEE.

COLORS OF THE 11th INDEPENDENT BATTERY, N. Y. S. V.

Four Flags.

---

1. *National Flag*, silk.
2. *Regimental Banner*, yellow silk; painted with portrait of General HAVELOCK, and inscribed, "Havelock Battery, N. Y. S. V;" "Jehovah Nisi."
3. *Guidon*; inscribed by authority with the names of the battles in which the Battery had participated, up to the close of December, 1862, viz.: "Manassas, Chantilly, Mine Run, Gettysburg, Bristow Station, Chancellorsville, Rappahannock and Fredericksburgh."
4. *Guidon*, silk; originally inscribed with number of Battery in field. Returned to the Adjutant-General on the muster out of the Battery.

The 11th, or "Havelock Battery," was raised in Albany, under the auspices of the Young Men's Christian Association. It went out in the fall of 1861, reënlisted in 1864, served in all the principal campaigns of the war, and was mustered out in June, of the present year.

COLORS OF THE 12th INDEPENDENT BATTERY, N. Y. S. V.

One Flag.

---

1. *Guidon*, silk; new; with staff; inscribed in field, "12th N. Y. Battery;" on stripes, "Petersburgh," "Reams' Station," "Kelly's Ford," "Mine Run," "North Anna," "Tolopotomy," "Coal Harbor."

Returned to the Adjutant-General without history.

The 12th Battery was organized at Albany in January, 1862, from recruits raised in Albany, Troy, and Niagara county. It reënlisted as a veteran command in December, 1863, and in February, 1865, received thirty-two men from the 20th Battery by consolidation. With the exception of the campaign from May, 1864, to April, 1865, it was in the Artillery Reserve. The battles in which it took part are inscribed on its Flag.

COLORS OF THE 19th INDEPENDENT BATTERY, N. Y. S. V.

One Flag.

---

1. *Guidon*, silk; inscribed, Spottsylvania, Suffolk, North Anna, Coal Harbor, Weldon Railroad, Petersburgh, Hatcher's Run.

This Flag was returned to the Adjutant General, without history.

The 19th, or Stahl's Battery, was organized at Lockport in the fall of 1862, and was mustered out in June of the present year.

COLORS OF THE 26th INDEPENDENT BATTERY, N. Y. S. V.

Two Flags.

---

1. *National Flag*, bunting; upper red stripe and portion of field gone; original staff.
2. *Guidon*, national, silk; field and upper portion gone; original staff.

These Flags were drawn by the officers of the Battery from the Quartermaster's Department. They are much worn by continued service, and were in the actions of Cane River, and Avoyelles Prairie, La., and sieges of Spanish and Blakely Forts, Ala.

The 26th Battery was recruited at Rochester, under the synonym of "Barnes' Rifle Battery." It left for the field in December, 1862, and was in active service until the close of the war.

COLORS OF THE 27th INDEPENDENT BATTERY, N. Y. S. V.

One Flag.

---

1. *Guidon*, silk; one-third worn; embroidered with wreath and letters and figures, "N. Y.," "27;" accompanied by original staff; spear-head gone.

This Flag was presented to the Battery by Col. J. W. BROWN, at Camp Morgan, Buffalo, N. Y., Dec. 21, 1862. It was in engagements in the Wilderness, at Coal Harbor, and before Petersburgh from June 17, 1864, to April 2, 1865.

The 27th, or "Eaton's Battery," was recruited in Buffalo in 1862, and rendered good service in the field.

COLORS OF THE 30th INDEPENDENT BATTERY, N. Y. S. V.

One Flag.

---

1. *Guidon,* silk.

This Flag was returned to the Adjutant-General. It was furnished to the Battery by the Quartermaster-General.

The 30th Battery was recruited in the city of New York in 1861. It was a part of 1st New York Light Artillery Battalion, known as "Brickel's German Artillery," afterwards the 29th, 30th, 31st, and 32d Independent Batteries. It served in the Peninsula campaign, at Antietam and at Fredericksburgh, and in the Shenandoah Valley.

COLORS OF THE 1st REGIMENT CAVALRY, N. Y. S. V.

Twelve Flags.

---

1. *National Flag*, silk; worn, and a portion gone; plate on staff inscribed, "1st Regiment Cavalry, N. Y. S. V. V., 1863. Presented by the City of New York."

2. *National Flag*, silk; new; inscribed, "1st Regiment Cavalry, N. Y. S. V. V."

3. *Regimental Banner*, blue silk; new; on one side, arms of the State of New York; on the other, arms of the city of New York; inscribed "1st Regiment, N. Y. S. V. V. Cavalry." "Presented by the City of New York."

4, 5. *Guidons*, blue silk; inscribed "1st N. Y. S. V. V. Cavalry."

6, 7, 8, 9, 10, 11, 12. *Guidons*, silk; national; nearly new.

The Colors here presented were carried by the 1st Cavalry during its service, as a veteran command.

The 1st, or "Lincoln Cavalry," was organized in the city of New York, in the summer of 1861, under command of Col. ANDREW T. MCREYNOLDS. It was composed of seven companies (three of which were Germans) recruited in the city of New York; two companies, mounted and equipped, recruited in Ohio, and three companies, mounted and equipped, recruited in Pennsylvania. It left for the seat of war August 26, 1861, with over twelve hundred men. It reënlisted as a veteran command, in February, 1864, at which time it received from Brig.-Gen. JAMES C. SULLIVAN, the testimony that " the gallantry and zeal" which had been displayed by its officers and men, "on all occasions, and the promptitude with which they had discharged their duties, had been excelled by no other Cavalry Regiment in the United States service."

Represented by Col. A. W. ADAMS.

COLORS OF THE 2d REGT. "HARRIS" CAVALRY, N. Y. S. V.

Two Flags.

---

1. *Regimental Banner*, blue silk; embroidered with likeness of Judge HARRIS, "Harris Light Cavalry," and "In God is our Trust;" part of original staff.
2. *Guidon*, silk.

These Flags were returned to the Adjutant-General on the muster out of the Regiment.

Two Flags were presented to this regiment at Arlington Heights, December 5, 1861.* One, a National Standard, by Judge IRA HARRIS, in whose honor the Regiment was named; and one, an embroidered Banner, by Judge HENRY E. DAVIES, whose son, J. MANSFIELD DAVIES, was its first commander. The former was worn out in the field; the latter, the Banner here presented, was borne by the Regiment in all its wanderings and many hard fought battles.

On the 19th of July, 1861, Gen. CAMERON, Secretary of War, made the following order:

"J. MANSFIELD DAVIES, as Colonel; JUDSON KILPATRICK, as Lieutenant-Colonel; and HENRY E. DAVIES, Jr., as Major, are authorized to enlist and muster into the service of the United States at its expense, a Regiment to be called and known as the "Harris Light Cavalry."

---

*See N. Y. Herald, Dec. 5, 1861, and Russell's Diary "North and South," page 215.

The organization of the Regiment was immediately commenced in the city of New York, and was at first composed of two companies from Indiana, two from Connecticut, one from New Jersey, one from Pennsylvania, and two from New York. On the 15th of October, twelve companies had been recruited, armed, uniformed and mounted. The President commissioned the officers above named, and on the 20th of October, the War Department made an order, that the Regiment should thereafter be known and recognized as the Seventh Regiment of United States Cavalry. Congress having authorized only six Regiments of Cavalry, however, it was found that the assignment by the War Department could not be legally continued. An arrangement was then made by the War Department with Gov. MORGAN of New York, by which the Regiment was transferred to this State and entered on the Roster as the Seventh New York Cavalry, and as such the officers were commissioned by Gov. MORGAN. In December, 1862, it was changed to the Second New York Cavalry, but it has been more generally known by its synonym, "Harris Light Cavalry," which it took in honor of the distinguished Senator from this State, and as an acknowledgment of the interest which he had always manifested in its welfare.

COLORS OF THE 5th REGIMENT CAVALRY, N. Y. S. V.

One Flag.

1. *Guidon*, silk.

This Guidon was presented to the Regiment by the City of New York, in January, 1864, and was carried in the following engagements: Wilderness, Po River, Bowling Green, Hanover Court House, Ashland, Wilson's Raid, Reams' Station, Winchester, Fisher's Hill (back road), Cedar Creek, Nov. 12 (back road), and Cedar Creek, Oct. 19. Inscription, " N. Y. S. V., 5th Cavalry."

In the battle of Oct. 19, 1864, at Cedar Creek, Va., the 5th Cavalry captured twenty-two pieces of artillery, fourteen caissons, one battery wagon, seventeen army wagons, six spring wagons and ambulances, eighty-three sets of artillery harness, seventy-five sets wagon harness, ninety-eight horses and sixty-seven mules.

The 5th Cavalry, or "First Regiment Ira Harris Guard," was mustered into the service of the United States at Camp Scott, Staten Island, Oct. 1, 1861. It was composed of six companies from New York city, one from Massachusetts and Connecticut, one from Allegany county, one from Wyoming, one from Tioga, one from Essex, and one recruited in part in Orange county, New York city and Plainfield, N. J. Its first service was in the Provisional Brigade, Department of Annapolis. In March, 1862, it was assigned to the Department of the Shenandoah, under Gen. BANKS, and in September of that year, to Gen. HEINTZELMAN, commanding defenses of Washington. On the 23d of June, 1863, it was transferred to the Third Cavalry Division, Army of the Potomac. It entered the service with 1,064 men, and received 1,125 recruits at various times.

COLORS OF THE 8th REGIMENT CAVALRY, N. Y. S. V.

One Flag.

---

1. *Regimental Banner*, silk; embroidered arms of the United States, and "8th N. Y. Cavalry;" original staff, upon which, on silvered plate, is inscribed the names of officers killed in battle, and of battles in which the Regiment was engaged, viz.:

Col. B. F. DAVIS, Beverly Ford, June 9, 1863; Capt. B. F. SISSON, Belle Plains, Feb. 11, 1863; Capt. B. F. FORTE, Beverly Ford, June 9, 1863; Capt. B. C. EFNER, Beverly Ford, June 9, 1863; Capt. H. C. CUTLER, Beverly Ford, June 9, 1863; Capt. C. A. FOLLETT, Gettysburg, July 1, 1863; Capt. RICHARD TAYLOR, Richmond, May 12, 1864; Capt. CHARLES McVEAN, Stony Creek, June 29, 1864; Capt. JAMES P. SERAYNE, Stony Creek, June 29, 1864; Capt. JAMES McNAIR, Nottaway C. H., June 23, 1864; Capt. JAMES A. SAYLES, Nottaway C. H., June 23, 1864; Capt. T. S. FARR, Fisherville, Sept. 23, 1864; Capt. A. L. GOODRICH, Namazine Church, April 3, 1865; 1st Lieut. JAS. REEVES, Beverly Ford, June 9, 1865; 1st Lieut. CARL V. SMITH, Oak Grove, Oct. 14, 1863; 2d Lieut. JOS. ATWOOD, Roanoke Station, June 25, 1864; Color-Bearer JOHN KEHOE, Waynesboro, March 2, 1865; Color-Bearer NATHAN BOWEN, Five Forks, April 1, 1865.

Winchester, Harper's Ferry, Antietam, Snicker's Gap, Phillimont, Union, Upperville, Barber's Cross Roads, Amisville No. 1, Amisville No. 2, Freeman's Ford, Beverly Ford,

Middlebury and Upperville, Gettysburg, Williamsport, Boonsboro No. 1, Boonsboro No. 2, Funkstown, Falling Waters, Chester Gap, Brandy Plains No. 1, Brandy Plains No. 2, Culpepper, Raccoon Ford, Jack's Shop, Germania Ford, Stevensburgh, Brandy Plains No. 3, Oak Hill, Bealton Station, Muddy Run, Locust Grove, Barnett's Ford, Craig's Church, Yellow Tavern, Richmond Defenses, Meadow Bridge, Hawes' Shop, White Oak Swamp, Malvern Hill 2d, Nottaway C. H., Roanoke Station, Stony Creek, Winchester, Summit Point, Kearneyville, Opequan, Front Royal, Milford, Fisherville, Tour's Brook, Cedar Creek, Middle Road, Lacey Springs, Waynesboro, Five Forks, Namazine Church, Sailor's Creek, Appomattox C. H., LEE's Surrender, Danville Raid, Grand Review.

This Flag was presented to the Regiment by the ladies of Rochester, May 2, 1864. It was returned to the Adjutant-General, without other history than that inscribed.

The 8th Cavalry was organized at Rochester, Nov., 1861, under command of Col. SAMUEL J. CROOKS. It was composed of volunteers from the counties of Monroe, Genesee, Niagara, Ontario, Orleans, Jefferson, Seneca, Oneida, Otsego and Livingston.

COLORS OF THE 9th REGIMENT CAVALRY, N. Y. S. V.

One Flag.

---

1. *Regimental Banner*, blue silk; worn; embroidered with arms of the State of New York, motto, &c. Presented by Hon. REUBEN E. FENTON, in March, 1863, on behalf of the Ladies of Chautauqua county, and carried by the Regiment until July, 1864.

The 9th Cavalry was organized at Westfield, Chautauqua county, N. Y., in the fall of 1861. It was composed of companies recruited in Chautauqua, Wyoming, Cattaraugus, and St. Lawrence counties, and in the cities of New York and Albany. It took the field with 940 men, and subsequently received 1,591 recruits. During the campaigns of 1863-4, it captured the battle-flag of the 5th South Carolina Cavalry, at Trevillian Station; the battle-flag of 28th North Carolina Infantry, at Deep Bottom; the battle-flag of the 23d Virginia Infantry, at Winchester, Sept. 19, 1864; the battle-flag of KERSHAW's Division, at Middleton, Va., Oct. 19, 1864. It also captured 984 prisoners during the same period; and, in SHERIDAN's brilliant valley campaign, brought in forty-seven pieces of the enemy's artillery. Up to July, 1864, it had participated in over thirty fights.

This Flag is accompanied by the Flag of the 5th South Carolina Cavalry, captured by the Regiment at Trevillian Station, March, 1863.

COLORS OF THE 24th REGIMENT CAVALRY, N. Y. S. V.

One Flag.

---

1. *Battle-Flag*, silk; all gone but the fringe and a few tatters hanging from the staff.

This Flag was carried in the following actions, viz.: Wilderness, Spottsylvania Court House, North Anna, Tolopotomy, Coal Harbor, Petersburgh (June 17, 18, and July 30), Yellow Tavern (Aug. 19 and 20), Weldon Railroad, Poplar Grove Church, Boydtown Plank Road, and in every general engagement of the Army of the Potomac from May 6 to October 20, 1864.

The 24th cavalry was organized at Auburn in March, 1864, under command of Col. WM. C. RAULSTON.

COLORS OF THE 25th REGIMENT CAVALRY, N. Y. S. V.

Two Flags.

---

1. 2. *Guidons*, blue silk ; arms and motto of United States.

These Colors were returned to the Adjutant-General without history.

The 25th Cavalry was organized in the city of New York in the spring of 1864, by companies recruited in different parts of the State. A portion of the Regiment was from Hancock, N. Y., and was recruited under the synonym of "Sickles' Cavalry."

Represented by Lieut. F. J. EATON.

COLORS OF THE 1st REGIMENT DRAGOONS, N. Y. S. V.

One Flag.

---

1. *Regimental Banner*, blue silk; emblazoned with eagle and motto, "Semper Paratus," and "1st New York Dragoons;" inscribed, "Deserted House, Blackwater, Siege of Suffolk, Manassas Plains, Culpepper, Todd's Tavern, Yellow Tavern, Meadow Bridge, Old Church, Howe's Shop, Coal Harbor, Darbytown, Kearneyville, Trevillian Station, Newtown, Cedar Creek, Smithfield," and several names of battles so obliterated by wear of Flag that they cannot be deciphered — in all, twenty.

Returned to the Adjutant-General without history.

The 1st Dragoons was recruited in the counties of Livingston, Wyoming and Allegany. It was organized as the 130th Infantry, August, 1862; changed to the 19th Cavalry in August, 1863, and to the 1st N. Y. Dragoons in September of that year. The inscriptions on this Flag include the battles in which the Regiment was engaged while acting as Infantry.

COLORS OF THE 2d REGIMENT MOUNTED RIFLES, N. Y. S. V.

(One Flag.)

1. *Guidon*, silk; all gone, but part attached to staff and the fringe.

This Flag was carried by the Regiment while acting as Infantry, in the following actions:

Battle of Spottsylvania, May 21, 1864; battle of North Anna River, May 23, 1864; battle of Tolopotomy Creek, May 31, 1864; battle of Bethesda Church, June 2, 1864; battle of Coal Harbor, June 6, 1864; battle of Gaines' Mill, June 8, 1864; battles of Petersburgh, June 17, 18, 1864; assault on Petersburgh, July 30, 1864; bombardment of Fort Rice, August 17, 18, 1864; capture of Weldon Railroad, August 19, 20, 1864; battle of Pegram Farm, September 30, 1864; battle of Hatcher's Run, October 27, 1864.

It was carried during the campaign until July 30, by Corporal KEITH T. MCKENZIE, Co. I. On the 30th July, it was carried by Sergeant WILLIAM HUNT, Co. K. At the battle of Pegram Farm, Corporal MCKENZIE was wounded and the Flag was carried from the field by Sergeant WILLARD CARNEY, Co. E. At Hatcher's Run, it was carried by Corporal JOSHUA B. SMITH, Co. I.

The 2d Mounted Rifles was organized at Lockport, in March, 1864, under command of Col. JOHN FISK. In addition to the battles in which it was engaged, stated above, it served in the trenches before Petersburgh, and was under fire night and day from June 16th to August 15th, 1864.

COLORS OF THE 2d COMPANY SHARP SHOOTERS, N. Y. S. V.

One Flag.

---

1. *Banner*, silk; inscribed, "New York Sharp Shooters."

This Flag was presented to the Company by JOHN CLARK, Esq., on behalf of the citizens of Albany. It was the first Color in the Army of the Potomac that was planted on rebel breastworks, viz., at Mill Spring, 1862 — this Company being in the advance from Hampton to Yorktown.

The Second Company of the 1st Regiment N. Y. Sharp Shooters was organized in the city of New York, and left the State September 5, 1861, with 80 men. It participated in the following engagements, viz., Yorktown, Hanover Court House, Fair Oaks, Savage's Station, White Oak Swamp, Charles City Cross Roads, Malvern Hill, 2d Bull Run, Fredericksburgh, Chancellorsville, Gettysburg, Mine Run, Wilderness, Spottsylvania Court House, Coal Harbor, North Anna, Tolopotomy Creek, and in several engagements before Petersburgh. It was discharged from service August 29, 1864.

COLORS OF 1st REGT. ENGINEERS (SERRELL'S), N. Y. S. V.

Two Flags.

---

1. *National Flag*, silk; about one-fifth gone from end, center of nearly half of stars worn away; inscribed, "Vol. Engineer Reg.;" staff and cord and tassels complete; on ferrule are the words, "Presented by the General Society of Mechanics and Tradesmen of the City of New York, Oct., 1861."

This was the first National Flag that floated over Fort Pulaski, and also over Fort Wagner, after the surrender of those forts to the Federal arms.

2. *Regimental Banner*, blue silk; coat of arms of the city of New York painted in center, over which are the words, in scroll, "1st Engineer Reg't N. Y.;" under arms, in scroll, "Presented by the City of New York;" several rents across and a portion of center gone; staff and cord and tassels complete; spear-head broken off.

This Regiment (which is composed of representatives from almost every county in the State) was organized in the city of New York in the fall of 1861, by order of the President. In October of that year five companies reported to Brigadier-General T. W. SHERMAN, and proceeded to Port Royal, S. C., where, after the capture of Hilton Head, they were engaged in repairing and erecting fortifications. Five additional companies reported for duty in November and December, 1861, and in the fall of 1862, the Regiment was raised to twelve companies, embracing a force of 1,864 men. The several Battalions of the Regiment have participated in the following sieges and battles, viz.: Siege of Fort Pulaski; battles of James Island, Pocataligo, and Morris Island; sieges of Fort Wagner, Fort Sumter, and of Charleston; battle of Olustee; siege of Petersburgh; battles of Drury's Bluff, Proctor's Creek, Bermuda Hundred and the James, Honey Hill and Coosawhatchie. The principal service of the Regiment, however, has been in the line of its duties as Engineers, and in this respect it has performed an invaluable part and reflected high honor upon the State.

COLORS OF THE 15th REGIMENT ENGINEERS, N. Y. S. V.

Eight Flags.

---

1. *National Flag*, silk; worn and partly destroyed; staff, &c.
2. *Regimental Banner*, blue silk; embroidered with arms of the State of New York and motto, and "15th Regt., N. Y. S. V.;" original staff.
3, 4. *Guidons*, blue silk.

The National Flag and Guidons of this series were presented by the Common Council of New York city. The Regimental Banner was presented by Mrs. Col. BRADFORD.

5. *National Flag*, silk; new; inscribed, "15th Regt., N. Y. S. V."
6. *Regimental Banner*, blue silk; on one side arms of the city of New York, and on the other, arms of the State of New York; inscribed, "15th Regt., N. Y. S. V. Presented by the City of New York;" staff, &c.
7, 8. *Guidons*, blue silk; new.

These Flags were returned to the Adjutant-General, and are here represented by Maj. TIMOTHY LUBEY.

The 15th Regiment was organized in the city of New York in the spring of 1861, by Col. J. McLEOD MURPHY, under the synonym of "New York Sappers and Miners." It was mustered in as infantry and served as such from June to Oct., 1861, when it was ordered to report to Col. ALEXANDER, at Washington, for instruction as Engineers. In March, 1862, it was assigned to Gen. McDOWELL's command, and performed duties as Engineers in the Brigade commanded by Gen. WOODBURY. It was subsequently fully recognized as the 15th New York Engineers, with pay as such from Oct. 25th, 1861. On the 25th of June, 1863, the two years portion of the Regiment was mustered out, and the three years men organized as a Battalion. During the years 1863 and '64, it was recruited to a force of 1,832 men, and reörganized as a Regimental command. It participated as Engineers in every campaign of the Army of the Potomac, besides furnishing detachments to the Army of the James, and to the army under Gen. SCHOFIELD. It built bridges, felled trees, dug intrenchments, built redoubts, opened new roads, laid miles of corduroy, laid pontoon bridges, and performed duties that in the highest degree contributed to the success and to the safety of the army.

COLORS OF THE 50th REGIMENT ENGINEERS, N. Y. S. V.

Two Flags.

---

1. *National Flag*, bunting; with staff.
2. *National Flag*, silk; inscribed, "50th N. Y. S. V. Engineers; with staff.

These Flags were returned to Governor FENTON, and are here represented by Brevet Brig.-Gen. IRA SPAULDING.

The 50th Regiment was recruited in the middle and western parts of the State in July, August and September, 1861. It was organized at Elmira, under the command of Col. CHAS. B. STUART, and left the State on the 18th September. After a short service as infantry at Hall's Hill, Va., it was detailed to the duty of "Sappers, Miners and Pontoniers" (Oct. 22d), with orders to report to Col. ALEXANDER, of the U. S. Army, at Washington. It remained at Washington under instruction until March 19th, 1862, when it took the field with the Army of the Potomac. In July, 1862, it was fully recognized as a Regiment of Engineers on the same footing as the Engineers of the Regular Army of the United States. It participated in the Siege of Yorktown, and was then broken up into detachments with duties at different points in the Peninsula campaign, and in front of Richmond, and was with the Army of the Potomac in all its subsequent services. It laid all the bridges of the campaign of 1864, except the one across the James River, near Point Powhattan, in which work it was assisted by the 15th N. Y. Engineers. This was the longest military bridge ever laid. It consisted of one hundred and one pontoon boats, and was 2,010 feet in length. The Regiment was twice recruited prior to June, 1863; and, in 1864, it was again filled to its maximum of 1,800 men, with a surplus of over 200 men, who were assigned to the 15th N. Y. Engineers with which it was brigaded. It left the field with a record as honorable as that of any Regiment in the Army of the Potomac.

ORATION,

BY REV. E. H. CHAPIN, D. D.

FELLOW CITIZENS: I am truly grateful for the honor of being permitted, upon this memorable day, and this glorious occasion, to speak in the capital of my native State. I consented, however, to respond to this invitation, only because I felt assured that you could not expect any elaborate discourse. The historical facts, and the political principles with which this anniversary is associated, have been impressed upon the mind and the memory of the American people for eighty-nine years. On the other hand, such a review of these facts and principles, in their relations to our recent struggle, as shall be worthy to take a final place in the history of human development, and a philosophical interpretation of events, must be reserved for some more special occasion — at least for calmer moments.

The orator's present task is to give some expression to the spontaneous thought and feeling of the time. And yet how utterly inadequate, even for this purpose, is speech — much more the speech of any one man! The inexpressible emotion, the heartfelt conviction of the people, is the true testimonial of this day. The war-worn soldiers marching home; the "brows bound with victorious wreaths;" the "bruised arms hung up for monuments;" the shot-torn, cannon-scorched flags gathered in, like harvest sheaves among the storied trophies of the State — these furnish the rhetoric, the logic, the resistless eloquence of the hour.

But in such language as I may — not presuming to trespass upon your patience — I propose to devote a portion of my address to some reflections that naturally arise at this time; to say something in the way of congratulation, and to close with a few words of welcome and commemoration.

The truth which comes most prominently before my mind upon the present occasion, is expressed in what has been called "the logic of events." History assumes its adequate significance only when regarded as a grand intellectual and moral method — a continuous demonstration, of which God is the premiss and God the conclusion. A prior conviction of this truth would warrant us in assuming, what successive results confirm — the fact that principles never fail. Once planted in the soil of human nature, once fixed in the course of events, they are bound to work out their consequences. For the illustration of this fact, we may refer to three things associated with the present observance. Those three things are, the place, the day and the declaration.

We may, upon the present occasion, fitly remember that it was in Albany, that FRANKLIN, before a Congress representing a majority of the colonies, presented his memorable plan of union. The idea was not a new one. Long before that time it had been projected, and, at least, partially acted upon. Nor was FRANKLIN'S plan immediately adopted. The Provincial Assemblies thought there was too much *prerogative* in it, while in England it was considered too democratic. But from that hour, the idea of a perpetual union of the colonies became a definite object of thought, a living aspiration; and the illustrious patriot who foresaw, as in prophetic vision, the future grandeur of his country, lived to give his voice and his vote to the present Constitution of the United States. Thus the spirit of nationality, here summoned into life, marched with the steady "logic of events" from Albany to Philadelphia. Thus the fixed fact of 1787, assumed its majestic outlines here in 1754. And thus fitly may we associate the *place* in which we hold the present ceremonies, with the *result* which, on this Fourth of July, 1865, rises before us, reconsecrated by fresh blood, and which, by the struggles and sacrifices of the last four years, stands vindicated for coming ages.

Necessity fused the American colonies into one political organism. That early project of union was dictated by the condition of those colonies, exposed on every side to the encroachments of civilized ambition, and the hostilities of savage foes, and which could be rendered safe and strong only as the interest of each became the interest of all. It was in the perception of National Unity as the indispensable requisite of Popular Liberty, that that project grew into the confederation of 1778. And through the experienced need of a more efficient organization, giving unanimity to popular will, vigor and personality to national life, those germs of union finally ripened into the Constitution of 1787. Thus have the conditions of our national life been developed by the irresistible processes of destiny. Discarding the idea of accident, we can regard these laws of historical development only as procedures of the Divine will. Nations are not to be classed among the things that are *made*, but among the things that *grow*. That which is not of human invention may not be dissolved by human caprice. The colonies sown upon this continent were the forecast seeds of one great empire, which, if at first undiscernable to human eyes, were known and watched by Him who sees "the substance of things yet being unperfect," and by whom "they are in countinuance fashioned, when as yet there is none of them." Originating from different motives, and existing under various forms of political organization, they were nevertheless mostly composed of people of one blood, speaking a common language, and inheriting an inalienable birthright in the same glorious institutions. From the beginning, then, their affinities were far more radical than their diversities, and this tendency of common privileges was confirmed by common grievances.

But the incidents of our revolutionary struggle only furnished the *occasion* for an inevitable tendency. Nature, whose "order is a foreshadowing of that which is to be," has prepared this country for the abode of a united people. The organism of a continent knits us together, and forbids dismemberment. Mountains, whose spinal ridges running through latitudes, sustain but not divide the majestic framework of the land — rivers, whose springs are cold with arctic ice, whose outlets take the warmth of tropical summers, the throbbing arteries of four thousand miles — the indented seacoasts of the East — the incalculable riches of the West — the development of the inventive and hardy North — the spontaneousness and exuberance of the South, — these are the interdependent diversities that give to a nation an imperial unity, so that one member cannot say to another, "I have no need of thee," "and *I* no need of *thee.*"

And what has thus been prepared by nature, has been consecrated by history. We have acquired significance among the people of the earth, not by the actions of separate States, but by national achievements. Whatever occasions of local pride may exist, to whatever illustrious men or memorable records any State may lay just claim, these receive lustre from that to which they have imparted lustre—the entire Republic. The measure of honor is determined by what each part has done or given for the whole. Our themes of song and story, our deeds of renown by land and sea, our legends of labor and sacrifice and triumph in the past, our ideal for the future, halt in no sectional limitations, but sweep through us all with the inspiration of a common name. Geography may fix our battle-fields in Massachusetts, or New York, or Virginia, but history obliterates these land-marks, and incorporates them into one domain of national glory; nay, exalts them into areas of the world's long conflict, where a people contending for unity and independence, have achieved victories of liberty for the entire human race. The bones of our revolutionary fathers overlapped the lines of States and cemented the structure of a united Republic; and now the blood of their sons sprinkled far and wide, by the Mississippi and the Potomac, in the streets of Baltimore and around Atlanta, in the Wilderness and on the wave, on many a mountain ridge and in many a valley, from the walls of Sumter to the gates of Richmond, has rebaptized and reaffirmed the principle that has grown with our growth, and will not fail in our career—the principle of *one* nation, *one* flag, *one* destiny.

Those who in the obstinacy of the recent conflict have beheld, on the part of the North, only an outbreak of savage ferocity, or of national conceit, deserve no reply. Against specific instincts that will always reappear while human nature remains the same, we set the testimony of the general fact, that a more humane spirit has never characterized the annals of civil war. And if, in the unfinished work that lies before us, the popular sentiment errs it will not be on the vindictive side. We have been terribly in earnest to preserve the Republic. Yet reluctantly we accepted the challenge that struck at the nation's life. But, accepting it with a clear purpose, we have sealed and accomplished that purpose with dreadful but not too costly sacrifice. Who are to stand forth as our accusers? Shall they be the prevailing governments of Europe, their records crossed with furrows of blood and steeped in barbarous shames? They who have mercilessly warred, not only against rebellious action, but against dissenting opinion, giving confirmation to the words of HEINE, that "wherever a great soul has given utterance to its thoughts, there also has been Golgotha?" They who would conserve every finger's length of their own territory with lines of cruel steel, shall they condemn us for not surrendering the heritage of freedom to the desires of despotism? Well, we may expect that the functions of the critic will succeed the disappointment of the prophets, whose wishes have hardly yielded, bit by bit, as they were made aware of our triumph—in the first announcement of our success predicting an entire sheaf of after calamities, and sullenly falling back, as circumstances have emerged, with hopes that have grown "smaller by degrees and beautifully less," riding at full moon with the hosts of LEE, halving upon JOHNSON, quartering with KIRBY SMITH, waning to a ragged crescent with PRICE, and now resting as a nebulous outline on the intentions of NAPOLEON and the prospects of MAXIMILIAN.

Or will we be accused by that other spirit, that now stirs in Europe—a spirit of the age—the spirit of nationalities that to-day murmurs under guarded thrones, or in Italy leaps to glorious consummation? Does not that spirit approve our efforts to preserve our national existence — our exacting belief that the nation is more precious than the individual? Is it not sure that they will best respect the national life of others who have most strongly maintained their own? Is not the unlimited development of nations the condition from which evolves the brotherhood of the race?

Our work will vindicate our effort; the future will justify our sacrifices. We know that that work is not yet completed, although its bloody phases may have passed. We desire not only the form of the Union, but its spirit also. It is good, therefore, upon the present occasion, to invoke the memories of the earlier days when our fathers, moved by a common desire, were united in mutual love; when, as in the first Continental Congress, the hearts of all beat as the heart of one, and PEYTON RANDOLPH wept with SAMUEL ADAMS, as DUCHÈ led the prayer for "poor, devoted Boston;" when North and South spoke with a single tongue by LIVINGSTON and CHRISTOPHER GADSDEN and JAMES OTIS; when PATRICK HENRY exclaimed: "The distinction between Virginians, Pennsylvanians, New Yorkers and New Englanders are no more; I am not a Virginian, but an American;" when, for the Union with a zeal that may help to cancel her later history, first and foremost stood South Carolina. Such was the spirit of the past; shall it not be the spirit of the future? May the enthusiasm concentrated upon this occasion, resuscitating and illuminating these records of the former time, generate throughout the land an influence which, flowing into the bloody furrows of the war, shall prevail as a sentiment of nationality, in which alone there is lasting peace. In the meantime, we must accept what has come and what yet may come, as forced upon us by the "logic of events." Standing on this spot where the conception of our nationality was foreshadowed, now as it emerges from a transient eclipse, we may lament but have no reason to excuse the dreadful struggle which has settled, as we trust, forever, " the fundamental idea of our Constitution ; " " the political union of the people of the United States, as distinguished from a union of the States of which they are citizens."

Such, then, is the suggestion of the place. It suggests union. And now what is the voice of the day ? It is the voice of freedom. This is the anniversary of National Independence; it commemorates a public achievement, and invites us to contemplate the symbolized organization of a new government. But Liberty is not merely an abstraction in political institutions and expressed in the movement of a consolidated people. It is a real and personal fact. National independence possesses worth and significance only as it affords opportunity for the development of inward and spiritual liberty. On the other hand, it is a mistake to regard liberty as simply a private privilege. It is likewise a privilege for the State. A nation is free only as its individual members are free. As these rise in the scale of humanity, the nation grows great and strong. Every stroke of emancipation, every fetter snapped asunder, every man lifted up from social degradation to breathe the air, to feel the pulse of liberty, is a boon, not only to him but to the nation, an enrichment of its resources, an enlargement of its life.

Wisely, therefore, did the signers of the document which has just been read in our hearing, lay the foundation of their political action, in the inborn privileges of every human soul, and prepare the Declaration of Independence with the great affirmation that "all men are created equal," a doctrine that has been disputed—a doctrine that has been sneered at—nevertheless a doctrine that is supported by all the associations that hallow this day, and that is unfolded in the "logic of events." It is not this assertion that is visionary or theoretical, but rather the standards by which the proposition of equality is tried. If men are merely animals, the ethnologist refutes the doctrine with facial angles and skull bones; if the intellect is the test of equality, the philosopher refutes it by merely pointing at innumerable diversities of natural capacity. If social grades and appendages are to fix the decision, the despot both proves and makes his truism. But then these are not simply distinctions of race; they are individual differences which are found in all races, and are they to determine the claim to human rights and privileges? Are sensibilities to be attributed only to favorites of fortune, and are the refined alone to be enumerated in the moral census? Are the kings and rulers of the earth always the men of largest brain? Is civilized society organized upon the principle that only the strong shall be eligible and only the handsome shall vote? But these are assumptive standards, and do not furnish the test of equality. The criterion of humanity is not in physical structure or intellectual capacity or social development. It is in the possession of the Divine Image, the fact of a moral personality, the inheritance of limitless possibilities. These constitute the essence of manhood, and in these all men are equal. This is the fundamental point upon which the axiom rests. Admit this, and you may then estimate as you can what any man makes of the world, or what the world makes of him. Admit this, and you admit the lawfulness of every effort for freedom. Admit that there is a center of personality where, however dimly or feebly, the soul swings free, that may not be canceled by human ownership, or transmigrate into another's will, and you sanction the condemnation of every institution that narrows the scope of individual opportunity or paralyzes the springs of individual endeavor. Admit this, and you acknowledge the germ of the world's progress — the occasion of ancient controversies and successive wars — the seed that through ages has been growing, and shall continue to grow, until beneath the shadow of its foliage and its fruit, throughout the whole earth, there shall not remain one triumphant despot or one suffering bondman.

"The colonists are men," said JAMES OTIS; "the colonists are therefore free-born; for by the law of nature all men are free-born, white or black. No good reason can be given for enslaving those of any color. Is it right to enslave a man because his color is black, or his hair short or curled like wool? Can any logical inference in favor of slavery be drawn from a flat nose, or a long or a short face? Liberty is the gift of God and cannot be annihilated."

The sentiment of JAMES OTIS was the sentiment of the men who set that "self-evident" truth in the very front of their Declaration. Principles never die. They may be hindered in their work, or for a time covered up, but they must and will be accepted at last. Their logic is fatal to all inconsistencies, as well as to all falsehoods. Once assert this truth to serve a transient convenience, and it remains working in the world as an indwelling force.

Pontiffs, contending with secular dynasties, referred Divine Right to the people. Their occasion has gone by, but the

Divine Right of the people rises year by year. The Inquisition based itself upon the doctrine that the civil ruler had no power to punish heresy. The Inquisition has stopped, but the rights of conscience remain. The Puritan — Protestant of the Protestants — asserted the premises of Religious Liberty. He planted himself on yonder shores to secure that liberty for himself; to bar all other souls. But in vain did the persecuted turn persecutor. The logic of his principle shattered the limitations of his intolerance, and to-day, in all the land, is "Freedom in worshiping God."

So with the cause of liberty. It regards no political limitations, and smothers itself in no human devices. It has been long working in the world, and it is bound to accomplish its work. It has suffered from its foes, and it has suffered, perhaps, more from its friends. It has been the occasion of fierce and awful wars. For such conflicts it is responsible, as that divinest truth was responsible which brought not peace into the world, but a sword. It has engendered fanaticism, as what element of deep, rich life has not? The interest that elicits no exuberance is mean enough and flat enough for fools and slaves. The cause that has never made a fanatic, has never furnished a martyr.

Making not haste, taking not rest, the "good old cause" of liberty moves in the march of time, and developes in events. It is pushed forward by every increase of human thought, by every victory, and even by defeat. They who admit its premises must accept its conclusions. Magna Charta, the Bill of Rights, the Revolution of 1688, developed into the Declaration of 1776; and the Declaration of 1776, with its persistent logic and its assertion of equality, has been working through our history, has brought upon us a fearful contest, has burst out in a storm of blood and fire, until now it has culminated in this jubilee of 1865; and the voice of the day, speaking in the logic of events, is the voice of universal freedom.

The place and the day have attracted our thoughts to the great principles of union and freedom. It remains for us to consider the significance of the Declaration which has made this a memorable anniversary forever. Founded upon the doctrine of human equality, and therefore the inalienable right of every man to liberty, the practical effect of this great document was the establishment of a new and independent nation. The truth upon which this action proceeded was proclaimed in the assertion that "governments derive their just powers from the consent of the governed." The distinctive principle, then, which this paper brings before us, is the principle of popular sovereignty. The Declaration of American Independence is the great charter of democracy. Here was a decided affirmation covering the question that had been discussed so long and so profoundly; that had employed the minds and the pens of men like HOBBS and HOOKER, LOCKE and MILTON. Here was thrown into the arena of the world a challenge to ancient feudalism, and to hereditary thrones, distinctly and boldly asserting the Divine right of the people; the doctrine of WILLIAM LIVINGSTONE that "the people are the Lord's anointed." There is no time, there is no need, to unfold the pregnant logic involved in this assertion, to follow out the actual consequences that have changed the aspect of history, that are shaping the destinies of nations and of the race. "The Declaration of Independence," says GERVINUS, "has become the creed of liberalism throughout the world, and American institutions are in the background of every democratic struggle in Europe."

But I ask you to observe the *spirit* with which this Declaration was qualified — the considerate and solemn wisdom with which it was pronounced. Mark how far removed it is from all license, from violent haste; how eminently characterized by all that distinguishes a majestic and necessary revolution from mad rebellion. See how steadfastly it blends the idea of Liberty with the idea of Order. The principle of government is not desecrated, but reaffirmed in its true sanctity, while at the same time it is enlarged and ennobled. I ask nothing more than the document itself, with its long list of abuses, endured with "patient sufferance," its reference to constitutional attempts for redress, to repeated petitions, to humble appeals; its testimony to the reluctance and the yearning affection for kindred ties with which the final issue was approached. I ask nothing more than this to shatter the comparison which some have drawn between the conduct of our revolutionary fathers and the recent conduct of men who, with malignant treachery and guilty haste, have sought to cancel the very premises upon which those fathers acted, and to demolish the glorious structure which they built. To rebuke into the very dust the Rebellion of 1861, I invoke the Declaration of 1776.

And now as the Declaration stands vindicated and reaffirmed before the world, I refer to it with joy and with hope, as illustrating the great idea which has been working through the ages, the idea of true democracy, and the progress of the people in the organization of free government and the triumph of liberty and law. "The entire period," says another, "from the middle ages to our own, is filled with one constant struggle of democratic ideas which contend against the aristocratic ideas of those ages." The Declaration of Independence was based on precedents. It exhibits the character of gradual growth from ancient roots which distinguishes the evolution of everlasting principles, from reckless innovation and transient caprice.

It is just one hundred years since the Parliament of Great Britain passed the stamp act. That was a critical but not a creative instance. The sentiment of liberty which it affronted, and from which it elicited new force, was much, much older than the American Revolution, and will continue to develop results which that revolution in and of itself did not consummate. It was only a forward step in the progress of a principle that comes from remote ages, "scarred with the tokens of old wars," and whose majestic march is irresistibly onward. It has still many problems to solve, many antagonisms to encounter. Still it is feared and hated, discredited and opposed. VOLTAIRE's contempt for the people, more than a century ago, was echoed in the British Parliament but yesterday. But dreaded, contemned, opposed as it may be, the tendency proceeds. The steady current of five hundred years sets all that way. Every revolution, even every defeat, decides for the people. Philosophers like DE TOCQUEVILLE, while they are doubtful as to the fruits, prepare for the result. Kings suspiciously lift up the bayonets that "begin to think" to attract the electric shock from abuses that are doomed to fall; while friends of human liberty and progress in Europe still anxiously look to learn the development of the democratic principle in America.

Yes, fellow citizens, how is it with ourselves? We have accepted and reaffirmed this principle. We have set it forth anew, wet and fresh with our bravest and best blood. We have accepted this doctrine of the government of the people, by proving how it can be defended and preserved by the people. It has been ours to reassert our Fathers' Declaration, that governments derive their just powers from the consent of the governed. We hold the premises; are we ready for the conclusions? "Governments derive their just powers from the consent of the governed." There shall be "no taxation without representation?" In the assertion of this principle our fathers resisted the stamp act and threw the tea into Boston Harbor. How far shall we go in asserting it? Shall there be no taxation of property, and yet a taxation of labor and bones and sinews and thought and speech and the dearest human rights? Shall there be a taxation of any class of men while the men themselves are unrepresented? Shall they give their blood in the battle and their sweat in the field, and yet feel that they have no vital function in the organism of the nation? Shall we allow them the bullet but not the ballot? Fellow citizens, the principle that gives its distinctive character to the Declaration is the principle of universal suffrage. Understand me—that also is a principle that *grows* and does not madly *leap;* but to that conclusion it does grow. In my view, there is one condition to universal suffrage, and that is a condition which itself exacts—Democracy.

The condition of universal suffrage should be universal education. The condition of a man's vote should be, that he knows why he votes, and this will be enforced exactly in proportion as we understand what it is that votes. It is not corn that votes, nor cotton, nor greenbacks, nor a white skin, nor a red skin, nor a black skin. It is mind that votes. It is intelligent will that votes, or should vote.

Set your qualification here in educated fitness to vote, and the qualification will become universal, to the enhancement of the public safety and the public life. For this is a possible attainment. You can educate mind into intelligence, which is the ally and safeguard of Democracy. But you cannot educate color into black or white. In the meantime, with assurance as to the logic of events, let us remember that perpetual incapacity attends perpetual lack of opportunity, and that "a man only becomes fit for doing a thing by doing it." In the contemplation of our recent past, in the consideration of our future, the Declaration which has been read to-day suggests the significance, the triumph and the obligations of Democracy.

Fellow citizens: The subjects of our reflection constitute the themes of our congratulation. If MACAULEY truly impersonates the sentiment of those who won the battle of Ivry, how much more does it becomes us with joyful reverence to exclaim, "Now glory to the Lord of hosts, from whom all glories are." Surely the impulse of the present occasion is no mere sentimental excitement, but an overflow from every heart of emotions in which our patriotic gladness is mingled with the deepest currents of religious feeling. In the sunburst of our success we devoutly recognize the Cloudy Screen of His presence, who, in the night time of our adversity, has been to so many weeping eyes and to so many troubled yet trusting spirits a Pillar of Fire. Above the issues of battle we discern the God of our Fathers, whose own hand disposes conditions and determines events. And with no sanctimonious formalism, but with the irrepressible earnestness of the soul, we pour out our thanks to Him who has preserved our Union, who has exalted Freedom, and given victory to the cause of the people. And now, not only as the recipients but as the agents of those glorious results, most heartily do I congratulate the people themselves. I congratulate you upon events that have revived the original significance of this Anniversary. Perhaps many of us for the first time in our lives really feel that we cannot have too much Fourth of July.

We are sure that the most stupendous pile of rhetorical exaggeration cannot repress our enthusiasm or belittle the day. We are fully determined to celebrate; we cannot help celebrating. We are ready to accept the consequences; to snuff the smoke and the blaze, the saltpetre and sulphur, to have our ears deafened, our ribs compressed and our sensibilities trodden upon. Yes, let the land rejoice in all its summer beauty, for now there rests upon it the light of peace. Let the gladness of the people find expression in all lawful forms of demonstration. Let the flags, so lately draped in fitting mourning, now flutter amid the green leaves of July, in their floral contrasts of red, white and blue. Let artillery, with the entire diapason of its tones, wake every echo in the land. Let the appropriate joy be consecrated by the voices of sweet and holy bells. Let the hillsides burst into bonfires. Let the night-heaven rain with rockets from the setting of the sun to the culmination of the midnight planets. And let the popular recognition of the significance of this day, like summer air out of skies that have been cleared and freshened by the thunder, sweep down from woods on which the north star shines, until even the languid palmetto and the trooping magnolia shall stir with the ancient spirit and rejoice in it once more.

I congratulate the people upon the results of a labor which they so resolutely accepted, which they have so patiently borne, and which their efforts and their sacrifices have borne, and which their efforts and their sacrifices have crowned with success. I do not think that I am guilty of any unpardonable degree of exaggeration in affirming that the recent war furnishes a signal demonstration of the strength of popular institutions; the executive vigor that may abide in large masses of men; of their power to sustain the shock of national adversity; of their clear-sighted perception of principles; of their attachment not merely to liberty but to order — in one word, of the fitness of the people for self-government.

The grandest fact developed in our struggle has been the development of the people themselves. This has been the people's war, by them reluctantly engaged in. This is their triumph, by them this day gratefully celebrated.

It seems difficult for observers in Europe to comprehend the absolute identity of the people in this country with the government. The people are thus falsely regarded as a distinct class from the government. The soldiers are regarded as a distinct class from the government. The people and the government are one. If they had said the war must cease, by no possibility could it have been continued. It has been the war of the soldier, whose life-blood was the price of the legacy he left to his children. It has been a war that the government could not carry on in opposition to the will of the majority. With us it is impossible for the people to be opposed to the policy of the government in any matter of great importance. You might as well talk of turning the steam against the locomotive that is moved by it, as to talk of the people being opposed to the course pursued by the government here in this land.

One deep cause of our sorrow for the fall of our chief martyr — a sorrow that even to-day casts its shadow over our joy —

exists in the fact, that in him the people recognized a type of themselves, a clear apprehension of their purpose, a faithful execution of their will, the exact measure of their own steady movement towards necessary and righteous ends, equally distinguished from the conservatism that would anchor in unsafe moorings, and the radicalism that would drift without a rudder. It is with this indissoluble sympathy that they will mention his name to-day all over the land, with honor and regret. While in the spirit that so patiently and honestly accomplished its work, even unto the sealing with blood, they may recognize a spirit that was prevalent in all.

I congratulate the people, then, upon a reward which they have not only received but have faithfully earned. If any man can claim in some degree that honor which is due to him, "who never despaired of the Republic," that honor is still more eminently due to the great body of the nation.

And that honor is deserved by *you*, friends, fellow laborers in the great work of liberty and popular progress in Europe. You, who also in the darkest hours have "never despaired of the Republic." You, GASPARIN and GARIBALDI, and a glorious sheaf of others, "faithful among the faithless." You, RICHARD COBDEN, whose noble heart, now cold and still, would have so much rejoiced in our joy. You, JOHN BRIGHT, and GOLDWIN SMITH, and STUART MILL, we congratulate you upon this victory for our Union and for liberty, which is also a victory for the cause for which you are so gloriously contending.

And with these words of congratulation we mingle words of welcome. Welcome to — by what name shall we designate them? Shall we call them guests? No, not if that name implies the least significance of "stranger." Welcome soldiers, heroes, sons and defenders of the Republic. Welcome the general and commander of our army, whose name need not be spoken, whose deeds have made mere eulogy presumptuous. We welcome him, in whose clear and comprehensive mind from the first was printed the map of the entire campaign, and who "fighting it out on the line" of his steady purpose, has covered that map with the results. We welcome him in whom the genius of military achievement is seconded by the genius of a marvelous patience; in whom the modesty of the man, and the patriotism of the citizen, lend lustre even to the fame of the soldier. His welcome, not only now, but in all coming time, is as wide and sure as are the liberty and Union which he has so triumphantly served.

And we welcome, also, this long line of heroic chieftains, who will stand in historic renown as a chain of mountain peaks on whose summits the sunlight rests.

And with these, we welcome every faithful leader, every soldier — natives of our own land, natives of every land — who have poured and mingled their blood to complete the priceless pledge, the ensanguined heraldry of those great privileges which are for *all* nations.

This is a welcome that will be sounded to-day all over the land. Every loyal State of this Union will give welcome today to its bronzed and scarred and crippled sons, and will proudly gather up for the contemplation of other generations the memorials of their service and their fame; gather them up, not in the temper of sectional exclusiveness, but with the consecrating thought that the gifts and sacrifices of each have secured the welfare of the whole; that the blood and treasure of the State have preserved the life of the nation. In this spirit we recall the efforts and the contributions by which

New York has been distinguished in this war. Stop one moment at the first item, and consider how much liberty costs as it grows, and how its labors increase as its area widens. "The entire number of Washington's army, rank and file, present and fit for duty," on the 12th of June immediately preceding the 4th of July, 1776, was about seven thousand. This was the host that was to support the Declaration of Independence. The number which the State of New York alone has sent into the field, to maintain and confirm the principles of that Declaration, amounts to nearly five hundred thousand men.

And where have these men been, and what have they done? Ask those flags, and they will tell the story. Enumerate the bloodiest fields, the most decisive victories of the war, and how few will you find where New York soldiers have not fought, where New York soldiers have not fallen! Follow their footsteps where GRANT has led and triumphed; where SHERMAN has marched and conquered; where SHERIDAN has struck like lightning! Let the testimony to their valor and their achievement speak from Cedar Mountain and Lookout Mountain, from Antietam and Gettysburg, from Coal Harbor, from Ringgold and Hope Church, from Peach Tree Creek, from the Wilderness, from Fort Fisher, from Atlanta, from Savannah; from conflicts even to name which would be an oration; from the first hour of the war to the last; from the bloody day of Baltimore to the surrender of LEE and JOHNSON. And has it ever been considered that it was only by sordid elements and material greatness that New York earned her title of "Empire State?" That it was only because her metropolis was mighty in commerce, and her fields were rich with wheat? See whether she who has borne the title does not deserve the honor. For lo! her city's wealth has been transmuted into sacrificial gold, and her fertile harvest fields have yielded *men*.

The heroes returning from those fields we welcome, and they will find that republics are not ungrateful. But there are those who went with them and who will not return. These too are to be welcomed, but not here. They have been promoted. They have gone where the private's humble faithfulness shines brighter than the general's stars. They have fallen into the ranks of the defenders and martyrs of Liberty, whose memories move through the ages of history and "whose souls are marching on." Their graves lie thick and lowly. Time and nature will weave for them their consecrating processes. The southern soil that drank their blood will deal as kindly with their ashes; the southern dews will weep above them as gently as though they lay in their own village church-yards, and close by their northern homes. Grass and grain will cover them. Winter will decorate their resting places as with monumental marble, and summer will spread over them its flowers of red, white and blue. The labors of the husbandman may obliterate them, and in the peaceful years to come it may be difficult to discriminate the hillocks of the dead, but the power of their sacrifice will circulate in the life of the nation. And wherever our groups of heroes rest, there will continually rise a testimony glorious as that which spoke from the graves of Thermopylæ · "Tell the Lacedemonians that we lie here in obedience to their orders."

In the list of those from our own State who have fallen, we might appropriately designate the names of SUMNER and MITCHELL, of RICE and BIDWELL—but where would we end?

Many here, without being accused of invidious regard, will linger with tearful emotion upon the noble life and the gallant death of LEWIS BENEDICT. And the circumstance will excuse me for specifying, where so many might be specified, another memorable martyr of the State.

It was not merely that he sacrificed his bodily life from his convictions of duty and from his love of country — the poorest soldier who fell in the ranks has made that costly sacrifice; but that, holding as he did ample possessions, linking rich meadows with flourishing towns, and spread over many fertile fields, he rejected the allurements that might have appealed irresistibly to such as he. He felt that life was more than abundant opportunities for enjoyment and ease. He felt that *his* life was in devotion to principle, and that it was bound up with the destiny of the nation. Thus, those lands so marvelously rich by nature, so marvelously rich in fortune, will be richer now in history, and the beautiful valley of the Genesee will perennially blossom with the memory of JAMES WADSWORTH.

There are other martyrs concerning whom I dare not speak at length, lest the heat of a righteous indignation should dry up the genial charities of the hour. Wan, wasted, seared in body and in brain, they come up before us — those martyrs of the Southern prisons; whose lot has been more terrible than the lot of those who fell in the field, whose mental death and long drawn agony make merciful in comparison death by bullet and by steel. Fitly are they associated in our commemoration with those martyrs of our earlier history, martyrs of the prisons and the prison ships of Charleston and St. Augustine, the sugar houses of New York and those whose bones lay bleaching on the shores of Wallabout bay.

These gather around you, ye who have gone up from yonder cells of inexpressible, indescribable torture, and you are acknowledged as fellow laborers and fellow sufferers with them in behalf of the common heritage. Martyrs of the field, martyrs of disease, martyrs of the prison, yes martyrs of the *home*, too, whose hearts beat heavily under all this public joy, whose shadows and whose vacant places no festal light can brighten, to you we pay the tribute of commemoration.

And now let the Flags be gathered up and fixed in the archives of honor. Mute as they are, they are the true and eloquent orators of the occasion. Faded and torn, still they blaze with imperishable renown. They fan us with the breath of victorious battles. They have been wafted by the sighs, the prayers, the hopes of a struggling people. They have inspired the spirit of heroes. The souls of martys have ascended beneath their folds. Let them be gathered up, that our children's children may read from them the lessons of this critical yet glorious time. Let them long rest through quiet and prosperous seasons, as proofs and tokens that the true object of war is honorable and enduring peace; but ready, in peace or war, as loyal satellites, to follow "Old Glory," the Flag of the Republic, as under Providence, it leads and shall continue to lead, the upward and onward march of the Nations.

REMARKS

OF MAJOR-GENERAL D. E. SICKLES.

IN response to urgent and repeated calls, General SICKLES came forward, and when the long continued applause with which he was received had ceased, spoke briefly. He apologized for not speaking sooner, as he could not have done so without interrupting the order of proceedings prescribed for the occasion. After alluding to the soldiers who are returning to their homes, their high character and worth, and their claims upon the consideration of the government and the gratitude of the people, he said:

"Our country has shown in the war — now happily closed — that it has the will and the means to maintain its liberties and its nationality. The people have yet a high and patriotic duty to discharge, in contributing to the pacification and restoration of the Union. We will not heed the advice of nations that desire our dismemberment. We will not imitate England in her persecution of Ireland; we will not follow Austria in her immolation of Hungary. No! Our people will prove that they can not only put down rebellion, but that they can establish order in place of anarchy, and that they can restore loyalty where treason has hauled down its flag. How will we do this? By the justice of our government; by the magnanimity of our policy; and by charity in our own hearts. These sentiments will give that wisdom to our councils which will conquer all the difficulties and embarrassments of the situation. Our patriotic President and our chivalrous General-in-Chief have already invoked this spirit among the people. The President has shown us, in his wise measures of administration, an example of the means by which genuine amity can be established. And, if anything be wanting, let us seek the inspiration of the lamented LINCOLN. Let us build a heaven-high monument to that great and beloved magistrate, by adhering to the considerate and beneficent policy that we all know emanated from his generous and noble heart. He told us of his hope and aspiration for the future, in the concluding words of his last inaugural address. 'The time will come,' he said, 'when the mystic chords of memory, stretching from every battle-field and patriot grave to every living heart and hearth-stone throughout the land, shall swell the chorus of the Union, when touched again, as surely they will be, by the bettei angels of our nature.'"

FLAGS

RECEIVED SINCE PRESENTATION.

2d	Infantry,	One.
3d	"	Four.
5th	"	Seven.
7th	"	Four.
10th	"	One.
17th	"	Two.
39th	"	Three.
40th	"	Four.
43d	"	Three.
46th	"	Seven.
49th	"	Two.
51st	"	Seven.
59th	"	Four.
60th	"	Two.
61st	"	Two.
62d	"	Three.
63d	"	Two.
65th	"	Two.
66th	"	Six.
73d	"	Three.
75th	"	Two.
79th	"	Seven.
81st	"	Three.

91st	Infantry,	One.
93d	"	Three.
94th	"	Four.
95th	"	Two.
97th	"	Three.
98th	"	Four.
100th	"	Four.
102d	"	Five.
103d	"	One.
106th	"	Eight.
110th	"	Two.
112th	"	One.
120th	"	One.
121st	"	One.
124th	"	Three.
131st	"	Five.
132d	"	Four.
137th	"	Two.
143d	"	Two.
144th	"	Eight.
146th	"	Three.
152d	"	Four.
155th	"	Two.
157th	"	One.
158th	"	Eight.
164th	"	Three.
169th	"	Two.
170th	"	One.
184th	"	Four.
187th	"	Three.
188th	"	Two.

191st Infantry,	Three.
192d "	Two.
2d Cavalry (Black Horse),	Two.
3d "	One.
5th "	Eight.
12th "	Ten.
14th "	Nine.
20th "	Five.
22d "	Two.
1st Vet. Cavalry,	Two.
1st Frontier Cavalry, Co. K.,	One.
2d Mounted Rifles,	Three.
1st Artillery,	Five.
3d "	Seven.
5th "	Two.
6th "	Two.
7th "	Two.
9th "	Five.
14th "	Four.
1st Independent Battery,	One.
13th " "	One.
21st " "	One.
23d " "	One.
25th " "	One.
27th " "	One.
33d " "	One.
1st Engineers,	Four.

The above, with those that may be received prior to that time, will be included in the next annual presentation to the Legislature.

Printed in Dunstable, United Kingdom